ISRAEL

by Abraham Rabinovich

FLINT RIVER PRESS LTD.

1. "How fair are your tents, O Jacob, your encampments, O Israel! like valleys that stretch afar, like gardens beside a river, like aloes that the Lord has planted, like cedar trees beside the waters." (Numbers 25: 6)

2. Sand dunes in the Wilderness of Shur, in the Negev, Israel's southern desert. The Negev occupies some 12,000 square kilometers or about half of Israel's land surface. It was here that the country's first prime minister, David Ben-Gurion, planned that hundreds of thousands of Jewish immigrants from all over the world would settle, to bring about his vision of making the desert bloom again.

3. The arched aqueduct at Caesarea on the Mediterranean coast between Tel Aviv and Haifa... Built by King Herod in 22–10 B. C., it brought water to this important Roman coastal port that had no fresh water resources of its own.

4. Massada, King Herod's great mountaintop redoubt on the shores of the Dead Sea. The fortress was the scene of the last stand of 960 besieged Jews, under their leader Eleazar Ben Yair, who withstood the might of the Roman armies for three years. In A. D. 73, three years after the fall of the Temple in Jerusalem, they chose to die at their own hands rather than fall prisoner to the Romans. The austere rock has become a latter-day symbol of Israel's will to resist. Young Israeli paratroopers take their military oath on top of the mountain: "Masada shall not fall again."

ISRAEL

Text by Abraham Rabinovich

Originated and developed by
Nebojša Bato Tomašević

Designed by
Miodrag Vartabedijan

FLINT RIVER

FLINT RIVER PRESS LTD.

A Motovun Group Book

© Flint River Press Ltd, 1989

First published in Great Britain in 1989, by Flint River Press
Ltd. 26 Litchfield Street London WG2H 9NT
Distribution by: Philip Wilson Publishers
Ltd. 26 Litchfield Street London WG2H 9NT

ISBN: 1-871489-03-2

Text:
Abraham Rabinovich

Captions:
Asher Weill

Design:
Miodrag Vartabedijan

Photographs:
Werner Braun
David Harris
Garo Nabaldian
Richard Nowitz
Zev Radovan

Editor:
Madge Phillips

Production:
John S. Clark

Project co-ordination:
Una Tomašević

Color separation, printing and binding:
Delo,
Ljubljana, Yugoslavia.

FLINT RIVER

FLINT RIVER PRESS LTD.

CONTENTS

Introduction

A young Jewish artist fleeing Nazi Germany in the 1930s was persuaded by a wealthy friend in Prague to accompany him on a short business trip to Palestine before moving on to Paris. The friend was an ardent Zionist but the artist was not. Arriving in Jerusalem, the artist, increasingly unhappy at this Middle East detour, sulked in his Jerusalem hotel room the first day until he was pried out close to midnight by his friend, who insisted that he at least visit the Western Wall.

It was the anniversary of the destruction of the Temple in A.D. 70 by the Romans, and the space in front of the Wall was filled with devout Jews mourning that event as if it had just occurred. In one corner a small black-clad figure stood on a box, swaying back and forth in apparent prayer. Something about him caught the artist's eye and he drew close enough to listen. The man was not praying, but talking to God in Yiddish – the rich vernacular of European Jews. He was berating Him for the afflictions He had heaped upon his people through the ages and asking what was the justice of it all. On the way back to their hotel, the artist told his friend that he had decided not to sail back to Europe with him: "A place where you can argue with your Creator in Yiddish is the place for me." Fifty years later, he would still be in Jerusalem, one of the most acclaimed artists in Israel.

Since its founding, modern Israel has been engaged in an ongoing dialogue with God, its neighbors, its history and itself – a turbulent, electric dialogue that has made it one of the most vital nations on earth. A focus of world interest, it seethes with unfinished business. Not for nothing does this country with a population of only four million have the largest foreign press contingent after Washington and Moscow. Israelis themselves are hooked on the nightly half-hour television news magazine, which provides far more surprises and excitement daily than any Hollywood serial.

Israel's spiritual past is the heritage of half the world. Although poor in natural resources, it has been the subject of one of the most protracted struggles of our time between two peoples claiming it as their own. It is a land tense and contentious, but alive.

A young nation choosing to build itself in the mouth of a volcano, Israel tries to shape itself from powerful, often conflicting visions. It is a modern society attempting to come to terms with the tenets of an ancient religion, a western society trying to come to terms with the East where it dwells, a predominantly Jewish society planted in the middle of the Arab world and trying to come to terms with its own large Arab minority.

Modern Israel came to life only in the middle of the twentieth century, but it has a history 4000 years old. Its national posture is sometimes that of an imperial superpower, but it not infrequently seems part of the Third World. A mixture of Sparta, Oxford, the European ghetto and the oriental bazaar, it is a place that holds visitors in thrall. It will, in all likelihood, continue to do so for a long time to come.

Illustration of verses from the First Book of Moses: building the Tower of Babel.
The Works of Josephus Flavius, Strasbourg, 1581.

HISTORY

Before the Diaspora

In the beginning was the land bridge. Israel's position between Egypt and Mesopotamia, the two great centers of civilization in antiquity, played a central role in its history. Sometimes an independent nation operating in the gap between these superpowers, sometimes an ally or a vassal of one or the other, Israel learned to live in the middle ground. King Solomon took Pharaoh's daughter for one of his many wives to shore up his Egyptian alliance, and King Nebuchadnezzar took the Israelites as slaves to the waters of Babylon, where they would weep for Zion until permitted to return.

Long before the regional events described in the Bible, however, Israel had served as an intercontinental land bridge, a way station for early man, Homo erectus, emerging from Africa on his great trek to settle the world. At Ubediya in the Jordan Valley, archeologists have unearthed 1.4 million-year-old human remains, the earliest ever found outside Africa. The abundant stone tools and animal remains nearby indicate that Homo erectus camped here for many generations before continuing his outward march.

Forty thousand years ago, the land witnessed a confrontation as epic as any in recorded history. Remains found in recent years in caves in northern Israel provide the only evidence in the world of direct contact between Neanderthal Man, driven out of Europe by the last ice age, and a new species of human, Homo sapiens, thrusting up from Africa. They apparently did not make love — at least they did not interbreed, say geneticists — and no evidence has yet been uncovered to show that they made war. Yet within a very few thousand years, the more muscular Neanderthal disappeared and the more intelligent and agile Homo sapiens, the first modern man, conquered the world.

Ten thousand years ago, agriculture developed somewhere in the 500-kilometer strip stretching from Israel's Jordan Valley northwards as hunter-gatherers began to put seeds in the ground instead of eating them.

Thus, long before written history began to record its saga, the land that came to be called Israel played a central role in the story of mankind. From the invention of writing in Sumeria and Egypt some 5000 years ago, reconstruction of the story of Israel becomes a task archeologists begin to share with historians. References to the land are found in Egypt and in Assyria, but it is the Bible that serves as the principal historical reference point.

Israel's biblical story begins with the arrival of Abraham from Mesopotamia. Some scholars date the Patriarchal age to about 1800 B.C. The land was known then as Canaan and was dotted with independent city-states ruled by kings. The patriarchs and their families — whether real individuals or symbolic tribal figures — are described as shepherds who settled in the sparsely-inhabited hilly spine running down the center of the country, rather than in the plains and valleys dominated by the Egyptians. Remote from cities and trade routes, these shepherd people could develop a national identity in relative peace.

Drought, says the Bible, sent Jacob and his tribe into Egypt. The Exodus from Egypt is dated to the thirteenth century B.C. and the re-entry to Canaan to the twelfth. There is a lively controversy between those scholars who accept the biblical account of conquest under Joshua literally, citing certain archeological finds, and those who believe, on the basis of other archeological evidence, that the Israelites slowly infiltrated the land over generations before finding themselves strong enough to conquer it from within.

Precisely at the time that the Israelites were becoming dominant over the hill country after crossing the Jordan from the east, another people was invading the land from the Mediterranean to the west. The Philistines were among the 'sea peoples' pushed out of the Aegean at this time by an event historians are unclear about. The Philistines settled along the coastal plain, building five major cities. The clashes between Philistines and Israelites as they attempted to define the border between them figure prominently in the biblical story, the most famous being the skirmishes involving Samson. Although the Philistines were to disappear as a distinct people after several centuries, it is a derivative of their name that would be applied to the country through much of its ensuing history – Palestine.

The historical fog begins to dissipate with the capture of Jerusalem by David, who made it his capital. Archeologists supply the round date of 1000 B.C. for this event. As the history of the newborn kingdom overlaps increasingly with that of its neighbors who maintained records of their own, precise dating soon becomes possible.

If there is a golden age in ancient Israel, it is the 78-year consecutive reigns of David and his son Solomon. David, artful and daring, forged a nation from a collection of nomadic tribes and carved its borders with his sword. Solomon, born a prince, used statesmanship to exploit the gains won by his warrior father. Instead of making war against his neighbors, he married their princesses – 700 wives had he, says the Bible, not to mention 300 concubines. He also established highly lucrative trade routes. Hiram, king of the Phoenician city-state of Tyre in present-day Lebanon, was his principal ally in this enterprise. The Phoenicians, the most prominent seafaring people in antiquity, built for Solomon a merchant navy on the Red Sea, near the present resort of Eilat, that traded for gold and ivory in distant lands.

Hiram also dispatched to his friend cedar from Lebanon and skilled workmen to assist Solomon in the crowning achievement of his reign, the construction of the Holy Temple. David had bought its hilltop site for 50 silver shekels to provide a permanent home for the Holy Ark the Israelites had carried with them in their wanderings. The Israelites knew the Ark to contain the stone tablets Moses had brought down from Sinai and to be inhabited by the divine spirit. David's hands, however, had been too bloodied in war for him to undertake the Temple's construction. The task was left to his son, who carried it out on an appropriately monumental scale. The Bible provides an elaborate account of the Temple's construction upon the leveled hilltop. Solomon dispatched 10,000 men to Lebanon on monthly tours of duty, says the Bible, some to hew wood, others to haul it down to the sea, where the logs were tied into rafts and floated down the coast. In the center of the Temple was a small room, the Holy of Holies, in which the Ark was placed. The sanctity conferred upon Jerusalem by the construction of the Temple there would persist long after the building was destroyed, indeed unto this day.

The death of Solomon in 922 B.C. was quickly followed by national division. The ten northern tribes revolted against Solomon's heir, Rehoboam, who lacked his father's ability to handle people. The ten tribes formed a new nation which took the name Israel, leaving Jerusalem as the capital of the truncated state of Judah. Both states were centered on what in modern times would come to be known as the West Bank, Israel occupying the northern half known as Samaria. The two states fought each other intermittently for some 50 years before concluding peace. A period of prosperity followed for both kingdoms, so much so that the materialism and influx of foreign goods and tastes evoked warnings from the prophets of Judah that the nation was forgetting its religious values.

Title page of the book "Shulhan Arukh" (The Well-laid Table), published by Rabbi Joseph Qaro in 1555, from the 1698 Amsterdam edition.

This situation ended in 721 B.C. when the Assyrian army conquered the northern state of Israel, sending its people into captivity and settling a new population there. The fate of the 'ten lost tribes' was to be a subject of speculation through the ages. Twenty-one years later, the new Assyrian ruler, Sennacherib, marched with his hordes on Jerusalem, destroying cities along his way. In the Judaean king, Hezekiah, he found a formidable adversary. Alert to the Assyrian threat, Hezekiah started in good time to fortify his capital and secure its water supply. His engineers, working from both ends of the steep ridge upon which Jerusalem was built, hewed a tunnel through the rock to bring the waters from the city's only water supply, the Siloam spring, to a pool within the walls. A plaque placed there in Hezekiah's time to commemorate the event was discovered in the Siloam tunnel in 1880. It relates dramatically how the two digging crews heard each other through fissures in the rock as they drew close. ''. . . This was the way it was cut through . . . each man toward his fellow, and while there were still three cubits to be cut through [there was heard] the voice of a man calling to his fellow . . . The hewers cut, each man toward his fellow, axe against axe, and the water flowed from the spring toward the reservoir . . .''

At the same time, Hezekiah worked to shore up his people spiritually by introducing religious reforms and recruiting the prophet Isaiah to rally the population. The formidable Assyrian army laid seige to the city but was unable to take it. For another century, Jerusalem would remain at peace, but in 587 B.C. it finally fell to the Babylonian king, Nebuchadnezzar, after a siege of more than two years. The city and the Temple were destroyed and much of the population of Judah was deported to Babylonia.

This was the national trauma which elicited one of the most poignant of the biblical psalms. ''By the rivers of Babylon, there we sat down, yea, we wept, when we remembered Zion. Upon the willows in the midst thereof we hanged up our harps. For there they that led us captive asked of us words of song, and our tormentors asked of us mirth: 'Sing us one of the songs of Zion.' How shall we sing the Lord's song in a foreign land? If I forget thee, O Jerusalem, let my right hand forget her cunning. Let my tongue cleave to the roof of my mouth, if I remember thee not. If I set not Jerusalem above my chiefest joy.''

They did not have to wait much more than one generation. Half a century after Jerusalem's fall, Cyrus the Great of Persia conquered Babylonia and permitted the Jews who so wished to return to Judah. The returning exiles restored the walls of Jerusalem and undertook the construction of a new Temple on the ruins of Solomon's, but a much more modest structure.

It was King Herod, in whose reign, 500 years later, Jesus was born, who restored Jerusalem to physical splendor, indeed raised it to an unprecedented magnificence, as part of the staggering building program he undertook throughout his kingdom. His grandfather was an Idumean, one of an Arabic people who had converted to Judaism in the previous century. Perhaps the most controversial ruler the country has ever known, Herod executed many around him, including several wives and children and numerous other relatives and followers, in order to safeguard his shaky claim to the throne and stay in power for 33 years. He was, however, also a master builder, a leader with the vision and the administrative ability to push through some of the greatest construction projects the country was to know until modern times. Many of the most impressive remnants of the past admired by visitors to modern Israel, including the Western Wall and the Massada cliff-edge palace, are remains of structures built by Herod.

At Caesarea on the Mediterranean coast he created an artificial harbor by using astonishingly modern engineering techniques. Enormous blocks of granite, floated down the Nile from Aswan, were cemented together and sunk in 20 fathoms of water to form breakwaters. When new breakwaters in the modern Israeli port of Ashdod broke up under the pounding of the sea in the 1960s, engineers traveled up the coast to Caesarea to study how Herod's engineers had done it. Herod's Caesarea, the first major port on the straight coast, was capable of providing anchorage for scores of merchant ships and war galleys. On the broad moles built over the breakwaters were warehouses, hostels for sailors, and walkways where residents could catch the sea breeze.

The port city itself was a marvel of town planning on a grand scale. Archeologists have unearthed an extensive sewer system which was flushed by the tides and is large enough to drive a minibus through. They were able to validate the account of the historian Josephus, who wrote that the sewers "had no less architecture bestowed on them than had the buildings above". Public buildings were constructed of marble imported from Italy, and merchantmen sailing by would see a glittering white city. Like many of Herod's cities, Caesarea had a mixed population of Jews and pagans. The king therefore provided it with pagan temples, as well as a hippodrome for horse racing and a large amphitheater. The latter, excavated and restored, is today used for opera and concerts in summer.

Among Herod's other projects was a series of desert mountaintop fortresses at Massada, Herodium and elsewhere, built as potential places of refuge for himself and his court in the event of insurrection. Future generations of Jewish insurgents would find them useful bastions.

Herod's most notable building activities were in Jerusalem. The centerpiece of all his work was the reconstruction of the Temple and the platform on which it stood, the Temple Mount. The temple built by the Jews returned from Babylonian exile was far too modest a structure for his tastes. To restore it, 10,000 workers and artisans were mobilized by Herod, writes Josephus, along with 1000 priests who were trained as builders and craftsmen so that they could work in the areas of the Temple to which laymen were forbidden entry. Before construction began, masons spent eight years preparing the stones and transporting them to the building site.

First the platform built by Solomon almost 1000 years before by flattening the hilltop was doubled in size in a massive engineering project involving the construction of enormous retaining walls as high as 30 meters – the height of a ten-story building – and layers of vaults to support a vast esplanade over the steep slope. The Western Wall revered by Jews is in fact one of those retaining walls, the outer skin of the Temple platform but not of the Temple itself, which has completely disappeared. The esplanade created by extension of the platform was able to accommodate the masses of Jews who came from abroad each year on the pilgrimage holidays – as many as 100,000 on a given holiday – to join the Jews of Judaea in visiting the Temple.

Massive stones were transported from quarries for use in the project. One of them, 12 meters long, weighed close to 400 tons and is unequaled in size anywhere in the ancient world. Engineering faculty members from Israel's Technion, examining the Temple Mount construction after the Six-Day War, noted that by the standards of modern construction the walls of the support platform should be five meters thick in order to withstand the pressure. When archeologists were able to measure the wall's thickness, they found that Herod's engineers had made the same calculations – the wall was precisely five meters thick.

No less impressive than the engineering feat was the aesthetic accomplishment. Josephus, who was familiar with Rome and Athens, found the Jerusalem Temple unmatched for its beauty in the ancient world. The façade of the Temple, he wrote, "excited wonder in the eye and the heart". The Roman historian Tacitus, describing the siege of Jerusalem by the Roman army under Titus in A.D. 70, writes that Titus assembled his senior officers before the final attack, apparently on the Mount of Olives overlooking the Temple Mount. "It is said that Titus declared that the first thing to decide was whether or not to destroy the Temple, one of man's consummate building achievements. A few [of those present] felt that it would not be right to destroy a holy building renowned as one of the greatest products of human endeavor." The fact that battle-hardened officers, at the end of a long and bitter campaign, could consider sparing their enemies' most cherished edifice – especially, when it was common Roman practice to destroy the shrines of rebellious nations – is striking testimony to the temple's beauty and grandeur.

Although no extra-biblical evidence of Jesus' existence has ever been found, the description of the period in the New Testment fits in with much of what is known from historical and archeological sources. Money-changers, for instance, were part of the daily scene inside the huge basilica built by Herod at the southern end of the Temple Mount to accommodate commercial activities and administrative functions. Here, pilgrims from abroad exchanged their foreign coinage for shekels to purchase doves for sacrifice on the Temple altar. Although the basilica was outside the sacred precinct, many Jews resented commercial practices anywhere on the Temple Mount. This provides the background to the New Testament description of Jesus overturning the tables of the money-changers. "And Jesus went into the Temple of God and cast out all them that sold and bought in the Temple and overthrew the tables of the money-changers and the seats of them that sold doves and said unto them, it is written, my house shall be called the house of prayer but ye have made it a den of thieves."

The period seethed with religious ferment and Messianic expectations. Members of a small ascetic Jewish sect established a monastery-like commune on the inhospitable shores of the Dead Sea in the second century B.C. in the expectation that an Armaggedon-like war between the Sons of Light and the Sons of Darkness would expunge evil and permit them to impose their own ultra-strict religious laws upon Jerusalem. Armaggedon would indeed come for Judaea, but the results would not be what the Dead Sea sect had forecast.

Judaea had been a Roman vassal state since 63 B.C., when Pompey had taken Jerusalem. It had generally been a benevolent relationship, Rome initially permitting the Judaean kings to run their state virtually as they wished. From A.D. 6, however, the Romans imposed direct rule through regional administrators known as procurators. The procurator from 26 to 36 was Pontius Pilate. Roman policy was generally deferential to the Jews, with their peculiar demands. Unlike the other peoples within the far-flung Roman Empire, the Jews refused to accept any of the Roman gods into their Temple or to recognize the emperor's right to divine honors. They also insisted on not working on their Sabbath. The Romans agreed that sacrifices be made in the Temple not to the emperor, as was the practice throughout the empire, but on behalf of the emperor.

When the mad Emperor Caligula ordered the Roman governor of Syria, within whose jurisdiction Judaea lay, to erect a large statue of him within the Temple in Jerusalem, the governor, a brave official named Publius Petronius, first tried delaying tactics, since he knew the Jews would revolt before permitting the sanctity of their Temple to be violated. Finally, he wrote the emperor that the order could not be executed. Caligula dispatched a letter to Petronius ordering him to kill himself. Fortunately, word of the emperor's assassination reached the governor first.

However, a series of disputes with a succession of corrupt or insensitive procurators finally lit the fuse 20 years after Caligula's death. The Jews in Jerusalem revolted and defeated the local Roman garrison. When the governor of Syria marched on the city with a sizable force, he soon discovered that it was not large enough and withdrew to await reinforcements. The Jews ambushed his army in narrow mountain defiles as it retreated and overwhelmed it, bringing back to Jerusalem considerable weaponry. Recognizing that it faced a major revolt, Rome dispatched one of its best generals, Vespasian, with a formidable army. After subduing the northern part of the country, Vespasian was recalled to Rome to be proclaimed emperor. His son, Titus, took over command and in A.D. 70 appeared below the walls of Jerusalem with four legions. The Jews, split into numerous

factions, had spent the time before the Romans' arrival in bloody civil strife. Nevertheless, the defense was ferocious. In periodic sallies, the Jews disrupted the Roman deployment, once almost capturing Titus. After lengthy preparations, the Romans brought up siege machines to break through the walls, only to have them collapse into tunnels dug by the Jews or set aflame in daring forays.

After four costly months, the Romans finally succeeded in piercing the walls and capturing the eastern side of the city, including the Temple Mount. The battle was furious, with armed Temple priests joining the fray. According to Josephus, Titus had given orders to spare the Temple, but in the heat of the battle a soldier, standing on the shoulders of another, hurled a firebrand through an opening and the building was consumed. In the frenzy of the hour, the Romans destroyed all the other structures on the Mount, shoving their stones over the edge of the platform to crash on the streets below. They would be found there by Israeli archeologists nearly 2000 years later. The conquest of the Temple Mount did not end the battle. It was another month before the Romans could capture the Upper City of Jerusalem, the last defenders seeking escape through the elaborate sewer system.

The fall of Jerusalem in A.D. 70 terminated a millennium of Jewish statehood. But still the story had not ended. The Romans had crushed the backbone of organized military resistance but not the will to resist. Atop the flat-topped mountain known as Massada on the edge of the Dead Sea, a band of Zealots and their families continued to hold out three years after the fall of Jerusalem. The Romans laid siege and finally broke through the defense wall after building a huge ramp for their siege machines. Josephus, in his dramatic account, says that the Romans found everyone dead except for five small children and two old women, who emerged from hiding to describe what had happened. The leader of the Jews, Eleazar, seeing that the Romans would soon come through the breaches in the walls, called upon his followers to slay their families and then themselves. "Let us die unenslaved by our enemies and leave this world as free men in company with our wives and children." After killing their families, ten men chosen by lot killed the other men. One of these ten, likewise chosen by lot, slew the others and then impaled himself.

But still it was not over. One final twitch of resistance remained, a twitch even more violent when it came six decades later than the original uprising. Though the Romans had destroyed Jerusalem, Jews elsewhere in the country continued to live undisturbed. They were the majority in the land and maintained a vibrant communal life. Furthermore, they were backed by a powerful Jewish Diaspora, which constituted ten percent of the population of the Roman Empire. In 128, the Roman emperor, Hadrian, issued an edict forbidding circumcision. When he could not be prevailed upon to rescind it, the Jewish leadership in Judaea began to think about revolt. This time it would not be a spontaneous outburst, as it had been during the Great Revolt, but a carefully planned action.

First a massive armament program was secretly carried out, ploughshares beaten into swords. Recent archeological excavations have uncovered elaborate underground labyrinths dug by the rebels at strategic locations around the country as arms depots and troop assembly points. Unlike the Great Revolt, this one had a single leader. We know his name, Shimon Bar-Kochba, but little else. We do not know where he was born, how old he was, or what his personal circumstances were before he emerged as leader of the revolt that would bear his name. We do know that he was such a powerful figure that the leading sage of the period, Rabbi Akiva, hailed him as the Messiah. If he was indeed the effective head of the uprising from the planning stage through the armed conflict, then he must have been a strategist and tactician of the first order. In the 1960s, battle dispatches from Bar-Kochba himself, written on papyrus to two of his field commanders, were found by archeologists in a cave in the Judaean Desert in a state of remarkable preservation. The personality that

Shabbetai Tzevi (the false Messiah) appeared in the Ottoman Empire in the mid-17th c. Illustration from an 18th-c. travel chronicle.

emerges from the letters is stern and threatening. "I call heaven to witness against me ... that I shall put your feet in irons." The letters indicate that Bar-Kochba and his men observed religious law punctiliously even in the field.

There were two Roman legions in the country when the uprising began in 132, one in Jerusalem and one near Meggido in the north. Both were defeated by Bar-Kochba's men. Reinforcements were dispatched from Transjordan, Syria and Egypt, but these too were mauled. The legion sent from Egypt, the 22nd, disappeared afterwards from the listings of military units published in Rome, leading scholars to speculate that it was cut up so badly that it ceased to exist as an organized force.

The successes were remarkable because, unlike the Great Revolt, these battles against the most powerful military machine in the world were not fought from behind protective walls but in close-in combat. The Jews, farmers turned warriors, apparently employed guerilla tactics, foraying from their underground lairs, ambushing convoys and striking by night.

These initial successes won the Jews a breathing space that enabled them to set up at least the rudimentary infrastructure of an independent state, including a coin mint, in the southern part of the country. It is these coins, with inscriptions such as "Year One of the Redemption of the Lord", which provide some of the most moving evidence of the desperate bid for freedom.

Hadrian sent for the best commander in the Roman Army, Julius Severus, who was engaged in battle at the time in the hills of far-off Wales. Severus brought with him legions from the present-day lands of Britain, Switzerland, Austria, Hungary and Bulgaria. By 134, there were 60,000 legionaries in the country, an extraordinary number for a single campaign. Severus nevertheless proceeded cautiously. The Roman historian Dio Cassius writes that Severus' preferred tactic was to surround Jewish strongholds and starve them out.

We know of none of the sites at which the two sides met in battle except for the last one, Bethar, a large village in the hills southwest of Jerusalem. It is not clear whether Bar-Kochba chose it for his last stand or whether he was trapped there. Brief references in talmudic and Christian sources indicate that the siege lasted well over a year. When the stronghold fell, it was only after starvation and thirst had taken their toll. In the general carnage that followed, Bar-Kochba met his death.

So heavy were the Roman losses in the campaign that Severus, upon returning to Rome to report to the Senate, omitted from his address the customary formula: "I and my army are well."

A Roman historian reports that 580,000 Jews perished by the sword in the uprising, in addition to the many who succumbed to starvation and disease. The bulk of the population of Judaea is believed to have died, more perhaps than in the Great Revolt. For the survivors, the Bar-Kochba insurrection marked the great divide between nationhood and dispersal. Although a vigorous Jewish communal presence reasserted itself in Galilee within a decade, by the following century the Jews would be a minority in the land, and a steadily declining one. For the first time since Joshua and the Hebrew tribes had forded the Jordan 14 centuries before, the country ceased to be the Jewish homeland. Hebrew soon ceased to be a living language, giving way to the Aramaic spoken in the region.

Hadrian took revenge on the Jews by changing the name of the country from Judaea to Syria Palestina, and Palestine it would remain down to this century. The Romans plowed the ruins of Jerusalem and built upon it a Roman city, Aelia Capitolina. On the desolate Temple Mount covered with rubble, Hadrian erected a temple to Jupiter and a statue to himself.

Illumination from the Turkish manuscript. Zubdat al-Tawarikh. 1583. showing Abraham about to sacrifice Ishmael, with a genealogy of the children of Ishmael below.

The Jews went into an exile that was to last until the twentieth century. When they returned, they would put in the Israel Museum a bronze bust of Hadrian found beneath a kibbutz field, his stern visage no longer a threat but a relic of a long-vanished empire.

Emperors and Caliphs

An unusual silence descended over the ravaged country in the wake of the Bar-Kochba revolt. Jerusalem, or Aelia Capitolina, was little more than a military camp for the 10th Legion garrisoning this part of Palestine. The legion ensured that no Jews returned to their holy city except for one day a year. But the seeds of the next stage in the country's history were germinating in Europe and western Asia, where the followers of Jesus were steadily winning disciples. In the fourth century, with the conversion of the Roman emperor, Constantine, Christianity emerged as the official state religion. The emperor now ruled not from Rome but from Byzantium, renamed Constantinople (today's Istanbul), and the ensuing period of some 300 years would bear the name Byzantine.

The land began to stir with activity once again as it became the object of Christian pilgrimage. The permanent Christian clerical community grew as numerous monasteries and churches were built. Pious Christian families from the West, many of them wealthy, came to settle. Recent archeological finds in Jerusalem show that in this era it became a prosperous city with a broad colonnaded main street lined with shops. It is from this period that we have the earliest map of Jerusalem, a mosaic depiction found in the floor of a church at Madeba, in today's Jordan. The map shows the city crowded with large structures, evidently church institutions, as well as the colonnaded boulevard. Only the Temple Mount remained a desolate place, despite the structures built by Hadrian amidst the Temple ruins. This desolation was not disturbed because it was for Christians a confirmation of Jesus' prophecy of the Temple's destruction.

The entire country prospered during this period, both the rural sector and the urban. Agriculture was extended to areas it had never before reached, particularly the semi-arid Negev in the south. New cities flourished in the Negev as well. Caesarea reached its largest size under the Byzantines, with a population of some 100,000. In the centuries following the destruction of the Temple, Caesarea continued to serve as the capital of the Roman province of Judaea. During this period, the resplendent city took on an unexpected new role as a seat of religious scholarship for both Jews and Christians. Barred by the Romans from returning to Jerusalem, the Jews made Caesarea a center of learning with a renowned rabbinical academy. A Christian community had formed in Caesarea as early as the first century and the city was visited by Jesus' two great disciples, Peter and Paul. An important seminary and library were founded there in A.D. 231 by one of the fathers of the Christian Church, Origenes. Spared the passions of a holy city, Caesarea provided a tolerant climate for the pursuit of learning. Christian scholars in Caesarea compiling a translation of the Old Testament from Hebrew to Greek held extensive discussions with Jewish scholars in the city on the subject.

The period of Byzantine splendor was interrupted in 614, when the Persians invaded the land. Fifteen years later, the Persians were driven out, but renewed Byzantine rule was shortlived. In 638 an army which had surged out of the Arabian Peninsula only four years before, inspired by a new religion, laid siege to Jerusalem. The Christian authorities negotiated a peaceful surrender and the Moslem period began.

Caliph Omar was a generous conqueror. Upon entering the city, he visited the Holy Sepulcher, but declined to pray in it for fear that such an act would render it sacred in the eyes of later Moslems, who would seek to convert the building into a mosque. He then asked to be shown where the Jewish Temple had stood. Jerusalem had a special sanctity in

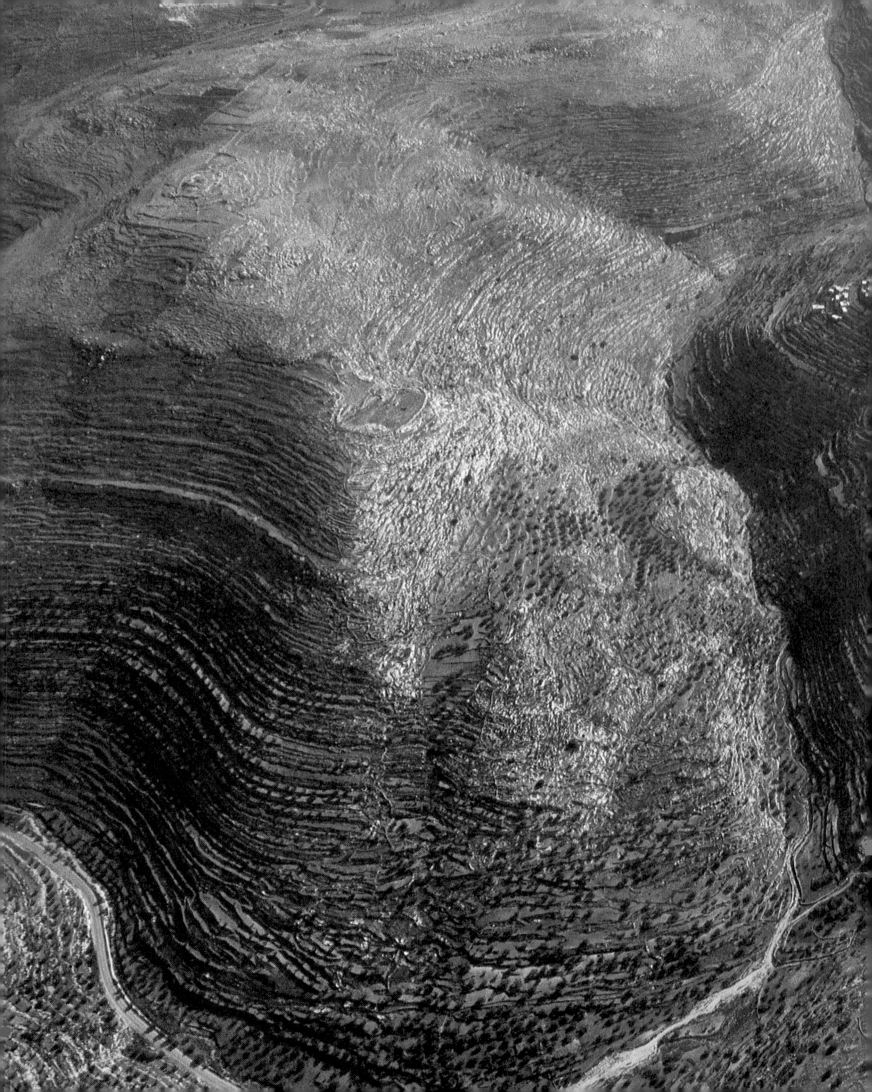

5. The Jordan winds its way southward from its source in the Hermon mountain range to Lake Kinneret – the Sea of Galilee – in the distance. To the right are the rolling hills of Galilee, and on the left, the steep escarpment of the Golan Heights.

6. The Dead Sea. The lowest point on the earth's surface, it lies 400 meters below sea level and is part of the Great Rift Valley, running from Anatolia in the north to Lake Victoria in Kenya to the south.

7. Salt deposits along the western shore of the Dead Sea. Its mineral products – potash, bromine, magnesium, gypsum, etc. – are a major source of fertilizers for the country and an important export industry.

8. Known in Hebrew as Yam Hamelach or the 'Salt Sea', the Dead Sea has 25% salinity – so dense that it is impossible to sink in its waters.

9. An Arab mountaintop village in Samaria, north of Jerusalem. Typically, Arabs settled the high places for reasons of defense, terracing the slopes for their crops.

10. Nahal David, a popular site for visitors at the oasis and nature reserve at Ein Gedi, by the shores of the Dead Sea. It was here that David, who had taken refuge from the vengeful Saul, caught the king unawares but refused to take his life (1 Samuel 24).

11. Ein Avdat, a deep natural pool of icy water in the Wilderness of Zin, in the Negev, not far from the last resting place of David Ben-Gurion and his wife Paula, at Kibbutz Sde Boker. The waters have turned the canyon in which Ein Avdat lies into a jungle of flowering plants and reeds, a refuge for the wildlife of the area.

12. A relic of the Six-Day War of 1967. Barbed wire entanglements still cling to this one-time Syrian gun site on the Golan Heights overlooking the settlements of Northern Galilee.

13.   An aerial view of Massada from the north. In the foreground is the three stepped Herodian palace. To the left, on the inaccessible, sheer, east side, a winding 'snake path' leads to the summit. To the west, the artificial ramp built by the Romans under their general Flavius Silva, from which they finally overcame the Zealot defenders, can still be seen.

14.   Kibbutz Ein Gedi on the shore of the Dead Sea. The foreground buildings belong to the Field School and lie along Nahal David running west into the mountains. The fields and buildings at the top (south) belong to the kibbutz.

15. Rolling sand dunes in the Negev, Israel's southern desert, near the Egyptian border.

16. (above) New settlements dot the hilltops in the mountainous region of Samaria on the West Bank of the Jordan River.

17. In the Kibbutz, there is time, too, for relaxation. Riding is a favorite pastine.

18

18. A newly-established moshav
(cooperative agricultural community)
nestling in the foothills of Mount Hermon,
Israel's loftiest mountain massif.

19. The green fields of kibbutz Tirat Zvi in
the Beit Shean Valley, south of the Sea of
Galilee, sweep down to Jordan. Across the
river lie the Mountains of Gilead and the
Hashemite Kingdom of Jordan.

20. Camels grazing at dusk along the Beersheba-Eilat highway.

21. At an experimental farm at Avdat in the Negev, scientists and farmers are attempting to recreate agricultural and water conservation methods used by the Nabateans, a people who successfully cultivated the Negev in the fourth to third centuries B.C.

22. A fisherman tends his nets on the Sea of Galilee.

23. Camels grazing in the summer scrub near Jericho. The trees in the distance frìnge the Jordan River, with Transjordan beyond.

24. The walled monastery of St Theodosius in the Judaean Desert, east of Jerusalem.

25. A wind-and-sand-eroded rock in the lunar landscape between Jericho and the Dead Sea.

26.   Part of the Dead Sea Works complex
at Sedom near the biblical site of Sodom
and Gomorrah. "Ten righteous men" could
not be found to save the doomed city of
undefined sins, destroyed by God "with
brimstone and fire" (Genesis 18–19).
Today, many hundreds of men and women
are employed here in one of Israel's most
important industrial complexes.

27.   Fresh water brought down to the Negev by the National Water Carrier has transformed the arid west bank of the Dead Sea into a major supplier of early vegetables for European markets.

28.   Mount Tabor rising gently in the dawn mist above the fields of the Valley of Jezreel in Galilee. On this site, inspired by the words of Deborah the prophetess, Barak assembled 10,000 men and defeated the Canaanites under Sisera. A millennium later, Jesus ascended the mount and, in the Gospel account, "was transfigured before his disciples". A Franciscan basilica on the summit of Mount Tabor commemorates the event.

Islam – next in importance only to that of Mecca and Medina in Arabia. On seeing the Temple Mount covered with ruins and refuse, Omar ordered the esplanade cleared and sprinkled with rose water, and on the presumed site of the destroyed Temple erected a small wooden mosque. replaced in 691 by the Dome of the Rock. Jerusalem was now a center for the three monotheistic religions. Omar likewise ordered that the Jews be permitted to return to Jerusalem.

The Arabs settled on the land and in established towns where the previous Christian and Jewish populations continued to live. The only city founded by the Arabs was Ramleh in the coastal plain, which served as capital of the region. In the coming centuries, the country came under the rule of different Moslem dynasties, and Arabic became the spoken language of all the inhabitants, regardless of religion. Despite periodic edicts limiting the freedom of Jews and Christians they generally lived peaceful lives under Moslem rule, and even served in government posts in certain periods.

Detail of the Latin text of the title page of the Emunot ve-Deot (Book of Beliefs and Opinions) by Saadyah Gaon, Amsterdam, 1647.

The Crusaders

A church council in Clermont, France, in 1095 heralded a new era for the Holy Land. It was at this gathering that Pope Urban II called for a Crusade to deliver Jerusalem from the hand of the Moslems. Tens of thousands across Europe responded. Some of those who set out the following year on what came to be known as the First Crusade were knights and holy men, but for the most part they constituted a violent peasant mob that massacred Jews and Byzantine Christians long before they reached the Moslem East. In June of 1099 the Crusader army arrived at the gates of Jerusalem. After a siege of little more than a month, Crusader soldiers stormed the ramparts of the walled city from a siege tower, and the defenders, Jews alongside Arabs, were massacred. Jewish civilians who had taken refuge in a synagogue were deliberately burned to death as the victorious Crusaders rampaged through the streets, putting virtually the entire population to the sword. The following year, one of the Crusade leaders, Baldwin, was crowned King of Jerusalem. The Crusaders' rule in Jerusalem would last only 87 years, but they would maintain a coastal foothold centered on Acre for another century.

Following the conquest of Jerusalem and the rapid subjugation of the rest of the country, most of the leaders of the Crusade returned to Europe. Those who remained behind recreated in the Holy Land a European-style feudal society, with nobles being granted tracts of land as fiefdoms by the king. For the country's largely Moslem rural population, Crusader rule meant little change. The level of taxation was no higher than it had been under Moslem rule, and the Crusaders left the traditional village leader to serve as local judge and conduct the community's daily affairs.

In the cities, the Crusaders either massacred or expelled the inhabitants and settled in their stead. A stream of immigrants from Europe soon filled up vacant houses. In the maritime towns, merchants from European mercantile cities such as Genoa and Venice, whose fleets had supported the Crusader campaign, were given entire quarters, which they

Illustration of verses from the Second Book of Moses: Pharaoh's daughter finds the infant Moses, The Works of Josephus Flavius, Strasbourg, 1581.

administered according to their own laws. The Crusaders built many churches around the country, some of them still in use, as well as fortresses which are today tourist sights.

Under the Crusaders, Jerusalem again became a capital for the first time since the Great Revolt 1000 years before. One of the major orders of Crusader knights, the Templars, made their headquarters on the Temple Mount and converted the Dome of the Rock and Al-Aksa Mosque into churches.

In 1187, the Crusader army lost a decisive battle to a Moslem army commanded by Saladin. Within four months, all the Crusader kingdom had been captured except for an enclave at Tyre, on today's Lebanese coast. Another Crusade headed by Richard Lion-heart, king of England, succeeded in winning back a strip of territory stretching down to Jaffa and re-establishing the Crusader kingdom, which existed until 1291 when its capital, the coastal city of Acre, fell.

With the return of the country to Moslem rule, Palestine ceased to be a subject of international concern for several hundred years. Nor did it play an important role in the cultural life of the Arab world. In 1516, the country was wrested from Egyptian control by the Ottoman Turks. The most dynamic force in Islam at the time, the Ottomans had in the previous century toppled Byzantium. A short-lived golden age now returned to the country as the Ottomans reorganized government administration and put an end to the insecurity that had been rife in the land because of brigands. It was the Ottoman sultan, Suleiman the Magnificent, who in 1437–40 rebuilt the walls around Jerusalem that still stand today. Following his death, a decline set in that would continue until the end of Ottoman rule in the twentieth century.

There was a brief incursion from the West in 1799 – exactly 700 years after the Crusaders' arrival – when Napoleon landed in Egypt in order to block Britain's route to India. He marched his army up the coast of Palestine, capturing all the coastal cities until he reached heavily fortified Acre. For two months his troops shelled and assaulted the town but the defenders, backed by the cannon of British warships lying offshore, withstood the siege. In the end Napoleon's army retreated to Egypt.

The West returned within a few decades, but in subtler fashion. Jockeying for positions of influence within the recumbent Ottoman Empire, nations like Britain, France, Germany and Russia opened consulates in Jerusalem in the nineteenth century and saw in the establishment by their nationals of church institutions, schools and hostels in the Holy Land a useful springboard for political penetration.

A revolution in transportation, the steamship, permitted the opening of regular sea links between Europe and the Holy Land by the 1830s. The telegraph arrived in 1865. In 1880, the population of the country was only 450,000, of whom 45,000 were Christians and 24,000 Jews. Palestine was still a poor, outlying province but the outside world was knocking on the door with increasing insistence.

Modern Times

Late in the nineteenth century, Palestine began to draw the attention not only of the European powers but of European Jews, for whom Jerusalem had been more of a spiritual than a geographic notion for well over a millennium. Anti-Semitism in central and western Europe, as manifested in the Dreyfuss Affair, drove many Jewish intellectuals, such as the Viennese journalist Theodore Herzl, to despair of true integration in European society and to weigh the possibility of recreating a Jewish nation in the ancient homeland. The seemingly unrealistic, indeed fantastic, aspects of such a romantic notion were offset by the desperateness of the situation, as they perceived it, and by the weakness of the Ottoman Empire.

The situation was more desperate for the Jews of eastern Europe, who were much poorer than their co-religionists in the West and subject to repeated pogroms. Even before Herzl founded the Zionist movement in Basle in 1897, small groups of young Jews from eastern Europe had begun emigrating to Palestine with the idea of becoming farmers and paving the way for a national renaissance. These pioneers, many of them students, aspired to a 'normal' Jewish existence centered on a return to the soil and physical labor. The immigrants found in Palestine a corrupt provincial administration, malaria and brigands.

Small groups within the old Palestinian Jewish community had rebelled against this way of life and, a decade before the arrival of the European Jewish pioneers, had established small agricultural settlements. In 1882, a year after serious pogroms broke out, the first group of Jewish settlers arrived from Russia. With the financial support of the French philanthropist, Baron Edmond de Rothschild, they established several farming villages. Small groups continued to immigrate, despite attempts by the Turkish authorities to stop them for fear of political demands the Jews might make if they gained strength. Hebrew, its usage confined largely to prayer since antiquity, was revived as a spoken language, and new words were coined for modern inventions and concepts. Following the abortive Russian revolution of 1905, several thousand immigrants arrived. Among this large group was David Ben-Gurion, destined to become Israel's first prime minister. These pioneers engaged in road-building projects and hired themselves out as farmhands. Immigrants also began to stream in from the other end of the Jewish world, Yemen, where Jews had lived in almost total isolation from their brethren for close to 2000 years.

Meanwhile, the new-born Zionist movement began to institutionalize these efforts to re-establish a Jewish presence in the land. A major tool was its Jewish National Fund, which began to purchase land around the country, often from absentee Arab landowners in Beirut and Damascus. Although much of the land was malarial swamp which had to be drained, other tracts were tilled by Arab tenant farmers, whose dispossession was a cause of grievance. In 1909, the first communal kibbutz was founded by a small group of pioneers on the shores of Lake Kinneret.

The First World War marked a major turning-point for the country. In the first three years, the Turkish army, supported by its German allies, used Palestine as a base for attacks on the British-held Suez Canal. In 1917, the British army under Gen. Allenby launched an attack from Egypt. Two weeks before Christmas it reached Jerusalem. Gen. Allenby, in deference to the sanctity of the city, dismounted from his horse at the gate to the walled Old City and entered on foot. Four centuries of Turkish rule had come to an end.

In November 1918, the British foreign secretary, Lord Balfour, issued a statement announcing the British government's sympathy with Zionist aspirations. ''His Majesty's Government views with favour the establishment in Palestine of a national home for the Jewish people... it being clearly understood that nothing shall be done which may prejudice the civil and religious rights of existing non-Jewish communities in Palestine...''

During the next 30 years, the attempt to give flesh to that brief statement by building a national Jewish home in Palestine was to cause growing friction between Jew and Arab.

Scenes from the Esther Scroll, Germany, 17th–18th c., copperplate engraving on parchment.

Jewish immigration in particular evoked Arab resentment. Armed clashes began between the two communities, and the British security authorities were hard put to maintain order. With the rise of Nazism in Germany, the tide of Jewish immigration substantially increased. A three-year period of disorder which began in 1936 came to be called the Arab Revolt, and the British at times employed tanks and planes to combat the uprising.

Faced with this irreconcilable conflict between Arab and Jew, the British dispatched a royal commission headed by Lord Peel to Palestine to recommend a solution. After hearing numerous witnesses, it proposed that Palestine be divided into Jewish and Arab states. Both the Jewish and Arab camps were split within themselves over whether to accept the proposal. They were rescued from the dilemma when the British dropped the plan in 1939. Facing the prospect of war, London did not wish to antagonize the Arab world. It issued a White Paper sharply limiting Jewish immigration to Palestine and restricting the sale of land there to Jews.

By this point, however, the Jews had built up the substantial nucleus of a national infrastructure, including an almost uninterrupted chain of agricultural settlements and towns from the Lebanese border in the north to the edge of the Negev Desert in the south. The Zionist movement had created a Hebrew-language educational system and two major institutions of higher learning, the Hebrew University in Jerusalem and the Technion in Haifa. An industrial and commercial infrastructre had likewise been established, as well as a health system and a trade union federation. A strong political leadership existed and, underground, an armed force as well. Taken together, these added up to a formidable state-in-the-making.

The Second World War paradoxically brought relative calm to Palestine, the internal struggle largely being suspended while the war raged. At war's end, the Jews began a massive effort to bring survivors of the Holocaust to Palestine, despite strict British immigration quotas. Most of the vessels engaged in this effort were seized by British warships and their passengers and crew interned in Cyprus. When one of these ships, the *Exodus,* was forced to return with its passengers to Germany, a world-wide uproar ensued.

In 1947, the UN voted to partition Palestine into two states, Jewish and Arab. The British announced that they would withdraw from the country on May 15, 1948. Fighting between Jews and Arabs broke out well before the British departure. In Tel Aviv on May 14 the leadership of the Jewish community in Palestine approved the Proclamation of Independence declaring the establishment of the State of Israel. At midnight that night, the British High Commissioner departed from Haifa and on the morrow five Arab states, unwilling to accept the creation of a Jewish state in Palestine, began to send armies across all the land borders to assist the Palestinian militias in their battle against the Israelis. The fighting continued with intermittent truces until January 1949. When it ended, Israel was in possession of 8000 square miles, compared to 6200 square miles allocated it by the UN's partition plan. Israel's War of Independence had cost it 6000 dead, one percent of the entire population. But almost 19 centuries after the Romans had destroyed Judaea, the Jewish state was reborn.

THE LAND

In the summer of 1867, Mark Twain and his companions on a donkeyback pilgrimage through the Holy Land pressed south through the hills of Samaria towards Jerusalem.

"The further we went, the hotter the sun got, and the more rocky and bare, repulsive and dreary, the landscape became," Twain recalled in *Innocents Abroad*. "There was hardly a tree or shrub anywhere. Even the olive and the cactus, those fast friends of a worthless soil, had almost deserted the country. No landscape exists that is more tiresome to the eye than that which bounds the approaches to Jerusalem."

If Twain were to return today, he would find it difficult to believe what the hands of man have wrought in a single century. The landscape has been transformed, not just on the Jerusalem approaches but from Dan to Beersheba, as the Bible designated the country's northern and southern boundaries. It has been softened with forests, contoured by the creation of rich farmland, and enriched by hundreds of rural settlements and by vibrant cities. Most of the country's 170 million trees were planted in the past 40 years alone.

It would take Twain only about eight hours today to drive the entire length of the country from Dan, a kibbutz on the Lebanese border near the site of biblical Dan, to Eilat, the southernmost place in modern Israel, almost three hours south of biblical Beersheba. It would take him less than an hour to drive across the country crossways, from the Mediterranean to the Jordan River. It would take only 15 minutes to drive across the country's narrow waist north of Tel Aviv where the West Bank foothills overlooking the sea define the pre-1967 border.

A small land by any standard, but with an astonishing variety of landscape, climate and ambience. A Jerusalemite, fed up with the cold winter rains lashing the capital, 800 meters above sea level, can get in his car and within 40 minutes be sunbathing on the shore of the Dead Sea, well below sea level, or lunching *al fresco* beneath a palm in a garden restaurant in nearby Jericho. The rain clouds coming in off the Mediterranean generally disgorge themselves by the time they reach the crest of the hill chain on which Jerusalem sits, leaving the low-lying area to the east sunny and warm. If the Jerusalemite chooses to descend the Judaean Hills to the west, he would within an hour be in the Mediterranean clime and metropolitan atmosphere of Tel Aviv.

If Twain were making that eight-hour cross-country drive today, it would take him from the ski lifts on the slopes of Mount Hermon to scuba diving in the crystaline waters off Eilat.

The map of Israel roughly resembles a hunting knife, the hilt being the hills of Galilee in the north of the country, the narrow upper part of the blade embracing the coastal strip around Tel Aviv as well as Jerusalem, and the broad part constituting the Negev in the south, with the tip of the blade resting on the resort of Eilat. The cutting edge would be the Jordan rift.

The coastal plain is lush with citrus groves, which thrive in the sandy soil. The sweet scent of orange blossom perfumes the region, even wafting into the area's towns. Farmers are reconciled to tithing a portion of their roadside yields to motorists unable to resist the temptation of plucking an orange or two from overhanging trees.

The high hills of Galilee and Judaea are covered mainly by pine and tapering cypress trees, planted on slopes too eroded for fruit trees or other crops. Olive trees thrive on the gentler slopes, particularly around Arab and Druze villages, where they constitute an important economic resource.

The dialogue between the desert and the cropland is one of the principal themes of the landscape. When the forested western slopes of the Judaean Hills crest along a line running between Jerusalem and Hebron, they give way abruptly to the naked hills of the Judaean Desert falling away to the east. From at least the time of David, this desert on the edge of Jerusalem was a refuge for fugitives and a nest for brigands. Visible from the ramparts of Jerusalem and the other cities atop the hills, the Judaean Desert fed the imagination and the imagery of the ancient poets and prophets, whose words are still read today. Jeremiah grew up in a desert-edge village just north of Jerusalem, and Amos in another just south of Jerusalem. The awe of the desert – and the awareness of the contrast between the dead landscape and the fertile slopes to the west – is clearly reflected in their visions.

There is a gaunt beauty to the desert hills. In winter, the scant rains which reach them are sufficient to tuft them with green vegetation and they are extensively grazed by bedouin flocks. The black goatskin tents of the bedouin are sited in areas sheltered from the prevailing winds. In summer, the bedouin move on to grazing areas in the north. As the desert hills approach the Dead Sea, they lose their gentleness and spawn deep canyons and precipices.

In the Negev, the transition from desert to cropland is less abrupt. The country opens up as one approaches the Negev from the north, with pines giving way to scattered palm trees, and for the first time there are horizons unbounded by mountain chains. The development of water resources sufficient to permit irrigation in this part of the Negev has pushed the desert back. Combines can be seen working their way through broad wheat fields. Gradually the farmland peters out and the landscape becomes an intractable waste of stony mountains and deep gullies.

In an hour's drive from almost anywhere in the center of the country, a visitor can encounter a dynamic modern city with high-rise buildings, traditional Arab villages dominated by graceful minarets, an ancient but still vibrant walled city like Jerusalem or Acre, collective agricultural settlements, ordinary small towns, and development towns settled by new immigrants in the 1950s in what was then the middle-of-nowhere.

There is relatively little urban sprawl, the towns and cities giving way abruptly to the countryside. The fact that the government owns more than 90 percent of the land makes landscape preservation easier. Strict limitations on roadside billboards prevent them from marring the landscape.

Each of the country's major regions has a specific character dictated by topography and climate, with sub-regions distinctively colored as well by history and demography. In antiquity, the relative isolation afforded by hill masses and valleys permitted the development of small city-states and tribal organization at a time when large empires were being formed in the flat expanses of the Nile Valley and Mesopotamia.

The country's western boundary is defined for much of its length by the Mediterranean, and its eastern boundary by the Afro-Syrian Rift, a great 4000-mile-long depression extending from Turkey to East Africa. The Jordan Valley is part of this rift or fault line.

Between the Mediterranean and the Jordan River lie the hills. In the north, they are the hills of Galilee, stretching virtually from sea to river. In the center of the country are the hills of Samaria and Judaea, set far enough back from the sea to permit extensive areas of settlement along the coast and inland foothills. This broad coastal strip is in fact the country's heartland. Atop the Judaean Hills stand Jerusalem and other biblical cities such as Bethlehem and Hebron.

The Negev in the south contains 60 percent of the country's land mass but only about three percent of its population. Most of it is rocky desert but there is plenty of semi-arid land which, with water and sweat, can be made highly productive. The western edge of the Negev is delineated by the Egyptian border, the eastern edge by the broad desert valley, the Arava, which is divided between Israel and Jordan.

The Jordan Rift offers some of the most gentle and also some of the most awesome vistas in the land as one progresses south from the Jordan Valley, where the river meanders slowly through rich farmland, to the point where it empties into the Dead Sea with its sulphurous breath and its rim of desert cliffs.

The North

The north is the most beautiful part of the country, by most people's standards. The rural, hilly landscape is a pleasure to the eye, particularly when the almond trees are blossoming or when blue lupins and red anemones carpet the slopes in spring. Arab and Druze villages predominate in the hill country. These villages were in centuries past built on high ground for better defense against marauders but they now sprawl down the slopes. Until recent decades, it was possible to see village women gracefully carrying jugs of water on their heads from the nearest well, but the advent of piped water has removed that scene from the landscape except in bedouin encampments.

Jewish farming settlements predominate in the once-malarial, now fertile, valleys and along the Lebanese and Jordanian borders, where they serve as security tripwires. Visitors

Illustration of verses from the Book of Daniel: the three young men rescued from the the fiery furnace, The Works of Josephus Flavius, Strasbourg, 1581.

to the border kibbutzim and moshavim can see the watchtowers and perimeter fences. One of the richest farming areas is the Jezreel Valley, scene of numerous biblical battles, which separates the Galilee Hills from the central (Samaria-Judaea) hill chain.

Beside their pastoral beauty, the well-watered Galilee Hills are also touched by religious and mystical association. Nazareth remains a focal point for Christian pilgrims, along with other New Testament sites, such as the hill overlooking the Sea of Galilee on which Jesus delivered the Beatitudes ("Blessed are the meek..."), Mount Tabor (site of the Transfiguration) and Cana village, where Jesus performed his first miracle, turning water into wine. Safed became a center of Jewish mysticism, the cabbala, in the sixteenth century and has retained something of that aura to this day in its old synagogues and picturesque alleys, some of which now comprise an artists' colony.

The centerpiece of the north, to which all eyes turn, is Lake Kinneret, the biblical Sea of Galilee. "I believe there are more beautiful lakes in the world, but I believe that there is not in the world a more fascinating lake," wrote one Christian author, gripped by its changing moods and gem-like setting. It is a lake first of all enjoyed from afar, offering stunning views at great distances and from numerous directions.

For Israel, the importance of the lake goes far beyond aesthetics. It is the country's only fresh water lake and its major water reservoir, draining a vast area that includes parts of south Lebanon and Syria. Water drawn from the lake is pumped through the National Water Carrier to the distant south, helping to turn desert land into flourishing fields. Reports on the level of the lake as it is replenished by the winter rains are broadcast regularly and followed with concern by the entire nation. Too low a level will mean limitations on irrigation. The Jordan enters Kinneret in the north and flows out of it in the south, at which point many Christian pilgrims perform the baptism ceremony.

Kinneret is also Israel's major recreational area, one whose importance increased enormously after Israel relinquished Sinai in its peace agreement with Egypt. Recreational parks have been developed on its periphery, but a favorite pastime for Israelis during holidays is to camp out on open sites along its shores. Much of the land around the lake is occupied by kibbutzim, which have developed guest houses and restaurants to accommodate tourists.

The main center on the lakeshore is the ancient city of Tiberias. Here one can enjoy a fish dinner on the water's edge while looking across the lake to the Golan Heights. A number of modern hotels have been built in Tiberias in recent years to meet the increasing winter tourism demand.

Overlooking the lake from the west are the Horns of Hittin, an extinct volcano where the Crusaders and the Moslem army under Saladin met in fateful battle on July 4, 1187. The Crusader army was moving to the rescue of besieged Tiberias when it was confronted at the Horns of Hittin by Saladin's force. The Crusaders numbered 1200 mounted knights and 20,000 foot soldiers, archers and pikemen. The Moslems, having learned that they could not withstand the cavalry charge of the heavily armored knights, effectively sidestepped them and cut the knights down with arrows once they were separated from their infantry. When the battle was over, all the Crusaders in the force were dead or prisoners.

The battle cost the Crusaders Jerusalem, but they would continue to maintain a foothold on the coast, centered on Acre, for another century. Although the city of Acre that we know today was built mainly in the eighteenth century, it still retains the outline and character of the Crusader city, and indeed still preserves many of the Crusader gates, watch-towers and dwellings. The most impressive Crusader remains in the city belong to the Order of St. John, known as the Hospitalers, who not only provided medical care for pilgrims and knights but were themselves a major fighting force. A subterranean complex in the Hospitaler compound, excavated in recent decades, includes the magnificent refectory with a 12-meter-high vaulted ceiling. Here Marco Polo probably dined with the knights before departing for the Orient. Stone carvings of the fleur-de-lys embellishing the room are the earliest known renderings of this emblem of French royalty.

The best example of Crusader city walls and Crusader streets are to be seen down the coast at Caesarea, where they were excavated in the 1950s. These walls, built in the thirteenth century by a late Crusader leader, King Louis IX of France, lasted only 15 years before they fell to the Mamelukes, a militant caste of freed Albanian slaves ruling Egypt. In 1940, Kibbutz Sdot Yam was established on the sands covering the ancient ruins. Although subsequently shifted to the periphery of the site, kibbutz members still occasionally unearth Roman statuary and other antiquities when land is plowed or drainage ditches dug. These relics of empire today line the walkways of the farming commune.

The major city in the north is Haifa, Israel's principal port and site of much of the country's heavy industry. The city is attractively situated on Mount Carmel overlooking the sea. Its reputation is that of a sober, tranquil, work-oriented city with neither Tel Aviv's flamboyance nor Jerusalem's grandeur. It is the only city in which public transportation is permitted on the Sabbath by local ordinance. The adjacent forests on Mount Carmel are among the loveliest places in the country for hiking and picnicking. A favorite Sabbath afternoon excursion is a drive to the shops and restaurants of nearby Druze villages on Carmel.

Driving inland from Haifa, one passes a roadsign reading Megiddo. Guarding a pass throught the Carmel ridge linking the coastal route from Egypt through the valleys leading towards Damascus and Mesopotamia, this was a site of numerous military clashes in antiquity. Solomon built a fortress here with stables for 500 horses. Its strategic importance was recognized in the First World War by Gen. Allenby, who maneuvered his forces there against the Turks and later took as his personal title Viscount of Megiddo. The biblical appellation Armageddon for, the site of the ultimate battle between the forces of good and evil, is derived from Megiddo with its long history of warfare. Today, it is a peaceful farming area.

The Center

A description of Israel's heartland is basically a tale of two cities – Tel Aviv and Jerusalem. Jerusalem is the nation's capital and its spiritual fount, but Tel Aviv is where the national pulse beats, the economic and cultural center of the country. Unburdened by the weight of history and religion, Tel Aviv's rhythm matches the urgent lapping of the Mediterranean.

Center of a large metropolitan area, the city lies on the coastal plain which in antiquity had been the home of the Philistines. To residents of austere Jerusalem, Tel Aviv is still Philistine, offering iniquities like pubs and discothèques and late-night cafés and strolls in the surf at dawn.

"Tell Aviv has become the vacation city of the Middle East since Beirut went under," says a city official. "You name it, we've got it." It would be an error for tourists to devote much time to Tel Aviv, but there is a vitality to the city that cannot be denied. There is also a muggy summer climate and an uninspiring, sometimes seedy, quality to the city's buildings. A recently built sea-front promenade is one of Tel Aviv's most attractive features. Jerusalemites visiting Tel Aviv feel almost as if they have gone abroad. Some of them who have moved to Tel Aviv, at least those who are not of a particularly religious bent, speak of a sense of liberation, as if they have emerged from some talmudical academy into a joyful parade. Tel Aviv women dress differently from Jerusalem women, walk differently, and return stares with a dead-on frosty sensuality. There is loose money in Tel

Aviv, and the speciality shops and art galleries that cater to it. There is also a lively theatrical and art scene and fine museums, including the Diaspora Museum with imaginative displays of the world-wide Jewish dispersion through history. As with other Mediterranean cities, a major pastime is sitting at sidewalk cafés and pondering the fate of the world as one watches the passing scene.

Tel Aviv was the first Jewish city to be founded in modern times. It was established in 1909 on sand dunes as a northern suburb of the largely Arab port city of Jaffa. The founders did not imagine that their small settlement would quickly become the urban focus of revived Jewish settlement in the country. Its dominant architectural feature for many years was a Hebrew secondary school, the first in the country and thus a proud symbol. In 1950, Jaffa, which had a mixture of Arab and Jewish inhabitants, was united with Tel Aviv into a single municipality. There is a rough-and-ready quality to Jaffa with its workshops and fish restaurants and flea market. The restored section of Old Jaffa overlooking the sea is today an attractive tourist area with restaurants and shops. Over the years, Tel Aviv has merged into a single conurbation with satellite towns around it, the total population numbering more than one million.

The history of modern Jerusalem is not much older than Tel Aviv's but it is a very different tale and it has produced a city of a very different character. Until little more than a century ago, Jerusalem was confined to the protective walls of what is today called the Old City. Roving bedouin bands and other brigands made it unsafe to live outside and the gates to the city would be shut at sundown.

It was a British Jewish philanthropist, Sir Moses Montefiore, who broke this permanent state of siege and began construction of the modern city outside the walls. The crowded and unsanitary living conditions of his co-religionists within the Jewish Quarter of the walled city made it apparent to him that they were more likely to die of disease inside the walls than from bandits outside. He purchased a plot of land a few hundred meters west of the walls and erected upon it a windmill, which he hoped would provide the first settlers on the site with a livelihood grinding grain. An architect was dispatched from London to design the residential quarter – two one-story buildings containing 26 apartments. The quarter was surrounded by protective walls and the apartments were offered rent-free for three years to needy residents of the Jewish Quarter, but the security situation made it difficult to find takers. Not even the name bestowed on the tiny quarter, Tranquil Dwellings, made it more alluring. For a long time, the families who finally did move in would stay there only by daylight, returning to the safety of the Old City at night. A number of residents did indeed fall victim to bandits in the early years, but slowly the security situation improved.

By 1870, the gates to the Old City were no longer closed at night. Other small Jewish neighborhoods began to sprout on the hills to the west, although these continued to be built with walls around them since their isolation made them vulnerable. These neighborhoods still stand today and are among Jerusalem's most charming quarters. The two original buildings raised by Montefiore – in effect, almshouses for poor families – have been converted. One is a plush guest house for visiting artists and writers and the other is a music center where young talents receive instruction from world-renowned masters in a program designed to compensate for Israel's distance from the musical centers of the West. The original windmill still serves as a landmark for the area.

At the beginning of this century, these extra-mural neighborhoods began to coalesce into a modern city, and well-to-do Arabs began to build housing outside the walls as well. The arrival of the British army in 1917 finally projected Jerusalem into the modern world. The city did not have electricity or a single motor car, but things swiftly began to change. The British introduced the concept of modern town planning and building regulations, and Jewish immigrants, particularly from Germany, spurred the development of garden suburbs. New types of building emerged – cinemas, coffee houses, large hotels, small industrial plants. Talented architects began to have an important impact on the cityscape. One of these new buildings, the distinctive YMCA, was the work of the man who a few years later would design New York's Empire State Building.

Tensions between Arabs and Jews in the mixed city flared up periodically over the years, even though many individual Arab and Jewish families enjoyed warm relationships. In 1948, with the outbreak of Israel's War of Independence, Jerusalem became the scene of some of the fiercest fighting. The Egyptian army reached a kibbutz at the southern edge of the city and was stopped only after the kibbutz had changed hands several times in desperate battle. Jordan's Arab Legion, attacking from the east, succeeded in capturing the Jewish Quarter in the Old City and some isolated Jewish suburbs, but could not penetrate the main part of the Jewish half of the city.

The war ended with Jerusalem a divided city. The larger, western, half was in Jewish hands and was declared by the new Israeli government as the capital of the nation. Jordan annexed the eastern half, which was smaller but contained most of the Holy Places, including the Western Wall and the entire Old City. The border between the two halves of the city was marked by barbed wire and minefields. The Hebrew University campus on Mount Scopus had been an Israeli-held enclave behind Jordanian lines throughout the fighting and it was to remain so for the next 19 years. Under the armistice agreement, Israel was permitted to maintain a garrison on the mount which could be rotated every few weeks in convoys escorted by UN military observers through the Jordanian half of the city.

A poignant peace descended over Jerusalem, each half going its own way but reminded by a stray glance across the line of the anomalous situation of a city divided against itself. Most poignant of all was the situation of the Arab village of Bait Safafa in southern Jerusalem, which was itself divided by the line. Half the village lay in Israel and half in Jordan, leaving members of the same clan suddenly living in different countries. For marriages and funerals, relatives and friends from the two sides would gather at the border line to celebrate or mourn together, with the fence still between them. The soldiers in the outposts on both sides would for a brief time overlook the rule against communication across the border.

The situation changed abruptly in June, 1967. Forty-eight hours after the first shots were fired in the Six-Day War, Israeli troops were at the Western Wall and Jerusalem was united once again, albeit by force of arms. Unlike the rest of the West Bank, East Jerusalem was annexed to Israel. In the post-1967 decades, Jerusalem witnessed what was probably the most intensive building activity in its long history. By 1989, the population had doubled to 500,000, of whom 72 percent were Jewish. Except for a few thousand Armenians and other foreign Christians, the rest were Arab.

The post-1967 period has also seen extensive restoration of old quarters, which has made them prime tourist sights. The Old City, whose infrastructure dated to Turkish times, received running water for the first time, as well as a modern sewer system and even cable television lines. The British in their master plans had called for the creation of a green belt around the Old City but had never been able to get rid of the numerous commercial buildings that had been raised against the outside of the walls near the Jaffa Gate, hiding them from view. During the period of the city's division, these buildings lay in no-man's land and became derelict.

Exploiting the euphoria of the immediate postwar period, Mayor Teddy Kollek ordered bulldozers to clear away these structures without awaiting formalities that could have taken years. At a stroke, the medieval walls of the Old City were once again revealed in their full grandeur. A green belt was created around the walled city and the ramparts were restored and opened to visitors.

In a large-scale beautification program initiated by the municipality, the stony city described by Twain was covered with vegetation: the roadways were lined by flower beds and trees, and the number of small parks increased in 20 years from 23 to 250. New cultural institutions mushroomed – a major theater complex, a cinemathèque, the world-acclaimed Israel Museum, and a host of smaller museums. Hebrew University, which had built a new campus in West Jerusalem during the city's division, reconstructed its Mount Scopus campus after 1967 in a major building undertaking that involved shaving eight meters off the top of the mount so that new buildings did not project too high into the skyline.

For the first time in its history, Jerusalem – top-heavy since antiquity with religious institutions and weighed down by an atmosphere of reverence – began to experience a vibrant secular culture of its own, not only through the imposing new theaters and museums but in a host of small halls and basements which became venues for theatrical and musical performances and lectures. This rising secular culture, however, was matched by a rising ultra-orthodox culture, and the two were not infrequently in conflict over such matters as the opening of cinemas on the Sabbath.

The Arabs of Jerusalem for the most part enjoyed unprecedented material prosperity, but coupled with a sense of political alienation. The prosperity was evidenced by a building boom and by the ability of young Arab men to marry much earlier because they could now earn sufficient money for a bride price with relative ease. These material advantages, however, did little to mitigate the awareness that they had been conquered in war. For Israelis, the moral dilemma of conquest was eased by the awareness that they had not started the war against Jordan. On a day-to-day basis, Arab-Jewish contacts in the workplace and marketplace were correct, often friendly. Arabs were sometimes elected to leading positions on works committees in plants with a mixed Jewish-Arab workforce. Jewish and Arab co-workers often attended each other's family celebrations, such as weddings, and on weekends Israelis thronged the Arab bazaars. But politically the Arabs of Jerusalem kept their distance.

Illustration of verses from the First Book of Moses: Joseph interprets the Pharaoh's dream, The Works of Josephus Flavius, Strasbourg, 1581.

As residents of territory annexed to Israel, they were offered the choice of Israeli citizenship or retaining their Jordanian citizenship. Overwhelmingly, they chose the latter, even when they worked for Israeli employers and received payments from Israeli national insurance. To ease the psychological and political pressure on Jerusalem's Arabs, the Israeli authorities permitted them to travel back and forth across the Jordan bridges to the Arab world. The authorities even agreed to the introduction of a Jordanian curriculum in the schools of East Jerusalem, so that Arab youths could qualify for the Jordanian matriculation exam and thus go on to universities in the Arab world if they so chose. It was a *modus vivendi* that worked more or less satisfactorily for 20 years until the uprising that began in December 1987 signaled that the Palestinian population was no longer willing to accept the political *status quo*. Whatever the outcome of negotiations, the experience at the human level of 20 years of daily co-existence in Jerusalem can be said to offer hope for the future.

The South

Before Israel's establishment, few beside bedouin tribes and hashish smugglers ventured across the southern Negev Desert. The torrid heat and barrenness offered little invitation to linger. Not even the Israelites under Moses had stayed long when they passed that way on their wanderings.

In the 1950s, the Israeli government decided that the empty map south of Beersheba must, for security reasons, be dotted with settlements. A small settlement had already been established at Eilat on the shores of the Gulf of Aqaba, with a few mad visionaries even predicting that the site might someday draw tourists. But between there and Beersheba, 200 kilometers to the north, there was only a tenuous road link.

The most logical site for settlement was the broad Arava Valley, cutting northwards from Eilat past the Negev mountains in a straight line to the Dead Sea. Though there were only three wells to succor travelers along its 180-kilometer length, test bores showed that more could be sunk. Since the Creation, this flat, sun-baked waste had never been farmed, but if settlements were to be established, they would have to be based on agriculture. In 1952, a settlement was established experimentally with a group of army youngsters at a place called Yotvata, 40 kilometers north of Eilat, where well-shafts had tapped an ample supply of water. Under the close guidance of agronomists, in time the settlers learned to farm the desert valley. First the soil had to be brought to life by washing the salt out of it. Then special crops were planted to provide the sterile soil with nutrients. A breakthrough was the development of drip irrigation, which supplied a measured mix of water and fertilizer directly to the plant through plastic pipes.

The area soon proved to have certain significant advantages. As there was no frost and crops were harvested much earlier than in the north of the country, higher prices could be asked for early vegetables that were virtually the only ones on the market. It did not take the farmers long to realize that even higher prices could be obtained by exporting their produce to Europe.

An experimental agricultural station was established in the desert valley. As experience accumulated, other kibbutzim and moshavim were set up in the area. For years these settlements had a tentative quality about them, with temporary-looking huts and a high turnover in personnel. The first residents were soldiers, young men and women serving in an army branch specifically aimed at training youngsters for settlement on the land after completion of military service. By the late 1960s, these quasi-military settlements had given way to permanent civilian settlements, a dozen of them scattered along the length of the Arava. As the new type of desert farming came to be mastered, the Arava farmers became among the highest income-earners in the country.

Such a success story had been envisioned by Premier David Ben-Gurion when he called on the country's youth to strike roots in the south. The south was Israel's hinterland – 60 percent of the national territory and virtually empty. It was wrong for two-thirds of the population to be crowded into the narrow coastal strip. It was necessary for national reasons, he declared, to fill in the map. He himself set an example when, upon giving up the premiership in his late 60s, he chose to start a new life in a Negev kibbutz, Sde Boker (Morning Field), as a manual worker. Though he did not succeed in inspiring a mass movement to the south, gradually the map did begin to be dotted with new towns. Beersheba, the capital of the Negev, grew from a small settlement into a sizable city with a university, a large regional hospital, a chamber orchestra and active theater groups. Other development towns were founded in the northern Negev with new immigrants, some of them trucked to the site directly from Haifa port upon arrival.

The most remarkable growth was in Eilat, which was discovered by European tour operators in the 1970s. Each winter, planes landing at the town's airfield disgorge tens of thousands of Europeans, mostly Germans and Scandinavians, looking for sun and sand, not holy sites or history. Scuba diving in the brilliantly clear waters resplendent with fish and coral was a special attraction. By 1987, Eilat had 4600 hotel rooms, with another 2600 in the pipeline.

Although the Negev is still far from crowded on the ground, an extraordinarily congested situation has developed in the skies above it. Following Israel's pullback from Sinai in the 1980s, its major air force bases were relocated from that vast peninsula to the narrow Negev. It soon became apparent to the planes going aloft on training flights that they were not alone up there. With alarming frequency, base commanders began receiving reports of collisions with flocks of birds or near misses. Such collisions often meant damage to the planes requiring extensive repairs, and sometimes caused injury or even death to the pilot when birds would smash through the cockpit. Within a few years, the air force was suffering far heavier losses to birds than it was to enemy action, even though the planes were periodically engaged over Lebanon. Between 1972 and 1982 there were hundreds of collisions, and damage amounted to tens of millions of dollars.

To understand what was happening, the air force command enlisted the assistance of the Society for the Protection of Nature in Israel (SPNI), which some time before had begun research into bird migration over Israel. It was a phenomenon which had never drawn much attention and little was known about it. A few hundred thousand birds, it was believed, passed over Israel each fall on their way south to Africa and each spring on their way back to Europe. Research showed, however, that many millions of birds were involved and that the bird traffic over the Negev was unsurpassed in the world except in the skies over Panama.

Birds from western Europe to western Asia funnel over the Negev on their semi-annual fly-past. These are mainly the larger species – eagles, pelicans, buzzards, storks. While small song-birds fly straight across the Mediterranean to North Africa in a single night, the heavier birds can not manage that long a stretch: they need to ride thermal currents, spirals of warm air that rise from ground warmed by the sun but do not develop over water.

With the problem thus defined, the air force set about solving it. The migratory routes of the different flocks began to be closely monitored – by ground observers, by radar, and by an observer in a glider that flew silently along with the flocks. Slowly a complete picture emerged. Each type of bird follows its own pattern, flying on roughly the same days each year, on roughly the same route and at roughly the same height. Rules were drawn up by the air force restricting training flights during the bird migratory period to specific routes and heights where planes were unlikely to encounter birds. Since these rules were formulated in 1983, the air force has not lost a single plane or pilot to birds, nor suffered major damage.

The Rift

Extending in a north-south line for more than 400 kilometers, the rift begins as kibbutz country in the fertile 'Galilee finger' thrust between the Galilee Hills and Golan Heights. Snow-capped Mount Hermon looms to the northeast, and in the fall the beautiful valley itself turns white as the extensive cotton crops are harvested. The headwaters of the Jordan rise here and a national park permits access to the newly emergent Jordan River, narrow but fast flowing, as it moves down toward Lake Kinneret. It is possible to splash down the small Jordan tributaries on rubber inner tubes provided by local entrepreneurs. The Huleh swamps, so laboriously drained by pioneers early in the century, have partially been restored – without the malaria – to serve as a nature reserve and bird sanctuary. Here visitors can watch from bird blinds as the large flocks land to rest during the migration seasons.

South of the lake, the river broadens to a width of some 30 meters, becoming the centerpiece of the Jordan Valley. It here forms the border between Israel and Jordan, and access to its banks is barred by security fences. There have been periods when border skirmishing kept residents in kibbutzim along the river sleeping in shelters every night for months, but in general Israeli and Jordanian farmers work their respective fields peacefully on either side of the river within sight of each other.

The river extends 100 kilometers south from Kinneret before it passes Jericho and empties into the Dead Sea. Situated 400 meters below the level of the Mediterranean, the Dead Sea – in reality, a lake – is the lowest place on the face of the planet. Waters that flow into it from the Jordan and smaller tributaries are evaporated in the intense heat, leaving behind a concentration of salts and other chemicals thicker than in any other natural body of water. Where ordinary sea water contains 35 g of salts per liter, a liter of Dead Sea water contains 275 g. So buoyant are the waters, that even non-swimmers lie on their backs in the Dead Sea and have themselves photographed reading a newspaper held aloft with both hands. The phosphates and other minerals extracted from the waters constitute one of Israel's most profitable exports.

At a remarkable oasis on the shores of the Dead Sea, Ein Gedi, a waterfall bursts forth from the cliffs and the desolation is displaced by thick shrubbery, trees and cool shade. In antiquity, David fled to Ein Gedi for refuge and an Israelite settlement was established there. The balsam perfume produced at Ein Gedi was prized throughout the Roman Empire, members of the settlement being sworn to secrecy about the method of production. A kibbutz has been established at the site and modern hotels have been built not far away at Sodom, at the southern end of the Dead Sea. The hotels cater mainly to Europeans suffering from skin diseases who find relief in the chemical-rich waters and mud of the Dead Sea.

Israel's portion of the rift valley ends at Eilat, but the deep, clear waters of the Gulf of Eilat, which follows the line of the rift towards Africa, teem with a wealth of colorful fish that makes it one of the choicest diving areas in the world.

There are few countries which offer such an astonishing variety of landscape, climate and mood within such a small space. So rich is this variety, so striking the contrasts, it is no wonder that since earliest times the dwellers in this land have pondered on the forces that shaped it and them.

29.   A Hanukkah menorah in a Jerusalem window. The Maccabees who liberated Jerusalem from the Greeks in 163 B. C. found a tiny cruze of oil in the plundered Temple. The oil sufficed to keep the menorah alight for eight days. The miracle is commemorated by Jews all over the world each year at the Hanukkah festival. The Arch of Titus in Rome shows a representation of the Temple menorah, the symbol of Jewish statehood, being carried off into captivity after the fall of Jerusalem in A. D. 70.

30.   The Old City of Jerusalem. A full moon hangs low over David's Citadel and the night-time traffic outside the Jaffa Gate. The Old City walls were constructed by the Ottoman ruler, Suleiman the Magnificent, between 1536–39.

31.   Jerusalem: city of three faiths. The Golden Dome of the Rock against a nightscape of churches, synagogues and mosques. The Western Wall lies behind and beneath the Dome. To the left is the Al-Aksa Mosque. The looming bulk of a luxury hotel on the right is actually well beyond the Old City in this foreshortened view.

32.   The moon hangs low over the Temple Mount. Jewish worshipers pray at the Western Wall in the foreground below the Dome of the Rock (center), and the Fortress of St Antonia (left) on top of the Mount.

33. The esplanade in front of the Western Wall, Judaism's most sacred site, and the only surviving remnant of the Second Temple. During the centuries after the fall of the Temple, Jews were only allowed to worship at the Wall intermittently and in limited numbers, and with the fall of the Jewish Quarter of the Old City to the Jordanian Arab Legion in 1948, not at all. With the liberation of the city in the 1967 Six-Day War, the Wall once again became freely accessible and is Israel's premier site of Jewish pilgrimage.

34, 35. The huge ashlars of the Western Wall rise 18 rows above the esplanade where the worshipers are standing. Jews of all degrees of belief and piety come here to offer supplications or prayers, whether soldiers on furlough or the ultra-orthodox Jews who form a small but highly visible section of Jerusalem's Jewish community.

36, 37.   For millennia Jews have prayed for Jerusalem. The Western Wall, the only remnant of Herod's Temple (destroyed by the Romans in A.D. 70), is Jerusalem's holiest site. The vaulted hall above lies alongside the wall. The old man (right) is placing a petition among the ancient crevices of the Wall.

38–40. The Western Wall (dubbed the
'Wailing' Wall by the British during their
Mandate) attracts Jews of all persuasions
and depths of belief. The man at top left is
wearing the festive fur hat known as
streimel, worn on Sabbaths and festivals.
The man on the right is wearing the leather
phylacteries or tefillin of early-morning
prayer. The man bottom left is wrapped in
his prayer shawl or tallit in accordance with
the biblical commandment.

41–43.   The Shofar, or ram's horn, is
another emblem of the State of Israel.
Blown by the high priest in the Temple in
ancient times, it is still an essential part of
Jewish liturgy at festivals. Sephardic Jews
(mainly originating from the Spanish
dispersion in 1492) favor a long, curled
horn. Ashkenazi Jews (mainly from Europe)
tend to use short horns. The worshiper in
the lower picture is holding a lulav (palm
frond) in his left hand, showing that this is
the festival of Succoth (Tabernacles).

44. Meticulously examining some of the ritual species required for Succoth, these orthodox Jews at Jerusalem's Mahaneh Yehuda market are carefully studying palm fronds and sprigs of myrtle to ensure that they are ritually perfect.

45, 46. Discussing the merits of an etrog or citron – a lemon-like citrus fruit which is one of the four ritual species required for the Succoth festival. The man below seems to be critically content with his choice of myrtle sprigs.

47. Reading the Torah scroll beside the Western Wall on Succoth. All four ritual species are visible in the picture: an etrog on the left, while the worshiper on the right is holding a palm frond, myrtle sprig and willow branch.

49

48, 51. This joyous group of Jews of Moroccan origin at the Western Wall is celebrating the barmitzvah of the boy who, with his father, is holding the round wooden container with the Torah scroll. Jewish boys enter manhood on their thirteenth birthday, when they are considered to have become fully-fledged members of the Jewish faith, able to take upon themselves all its privileges and obligations.

49, 50. The profession of a Torah scribe entails long and arduous work. The Torah, or five books of Moses, are painstakingly inscribed by hand on specially prepared sheets of parchment, which are then carefully sewn together and rolled up to form the sefer torah or Torah scroll.

52, 54, 55.   ''We were slaves to Pharaoh in Egypt, from whom we were delivered by the Lord our God with a strong hand and an outstretched arm.'' During the festival of Pesach or Passover, Jews eat only matza (unleavened bread) to commemorate the exodus of the Children of Israel from Egypt. The week-long festival opens with a family dinner called the seder, during which the Haggadah, the story of the Exodus, is recited by the whole gathering.

53.   The eighth and last light has been lit on this Hanukkah candelabrum celebrating the Maccabbees' defeat of the Romans and the recapture of the Temple in Jerusalem.

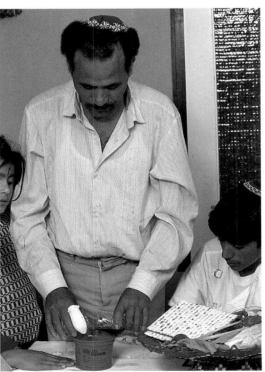

55

56. Mount Meron, ten kilometers west of the medieval Galilean town of Safed, is the burial place of several Jewish sages, including Hillel the Elder, Shammai and, above all, Rabbi Shimon Bar Yohai, a leader of the Jewish revolt against the Romans in A. D. 135. It is the site of a major pilgrimage during the festival of Lag B' Omer, after Passover. Traditionally, three-year-old orthodox Jewish boys get their first haircut on Mount Meron during this festival.

57. The traditional tomb of King David on Mount Zion, just outside the walls of Jerusalem's Old City. There is, however, no historical basis for this belief, and the tomb is probably that of an eleventh-century Crusader knight. Nevertheless, the site still attracts thousands of pious pilgrims.

58. The Shrine of the Book at the Israel Museum, Jerusalem, contains the Dead Sea Scrolls and artifacts from the Bar-Kochba revolt against the Romans of A.D. 132–135. The central display holds the scroll of the prophet Isaiah. The Dead Sea Scrolls are one of the most important sources of information on the early Christian era of the first to second century.

59. The traditional tomb of the matriarch Rachel in the town of Bethlehem.

60.   Orthodox Jews devote a substantial part of their lives to prayer and study. This man is leading his grandson through the morning prayers in a small chamber adjoining the Western Wall.

61, 62.   This group of Jews, originating from the Yemen, are seated on the ground reciting the prayers on Tisha B'Av, the ninth day of the month of Av, on which both the First and Second Temples were destroyed. (below) This man, deeply engrossed in his morning prayers, is wearing tefillin (phylacteries) on his forehead, arm and hand; this is an essential part of every observant male Jew's morning ritual.

63.   Night-time vigil at the Western Wall. The wall is attended by worshipers round the clock, and has never been deserted for even one minute since its reversion to Jewish hands with the freeing of the Jewish quarter of Jerusalem in 1967.

64.   Independence Day in Jerusalem. In Birket Sultan (Sultan's Pool), a huge amphitheater beneath the Old City walls, the choir of the military rabbinate participates in an open-air concert, while searchlights trace patterns in the night sky.

THREE RELIGIONS

Astroller through Jerusalem's Old City can sometimes hear 3000 years of history borne to him on a gust of wind carrying prayers from a synagogue, the pealing of church bells and the high-pitched call from a minaret summoning the Moslem faithful to prayer. Those mingled sounds illustrate the central place held by this remote Middle Eastern land in the consciousness of half of mankind, which perceives it as an earthly gateway between the now and the eternal. Jews, Christians, and Moslems have warred for it and prayed for it: its history and its stones are shared by these three great monotheistic religions. There is scant ecumenism to blur religious differences, but neither is there exclusivity, each religion acknowledging over the centuries that it must share its spiritual claims on the city and the land with other faiths.

To see over the course of a few days Jewish pilgrims crowding the Western Wall on Passover, Christian pilgrims filling the Holy Sepulcher Church at Easter, and Moslem pilgrims covering the Temple Mount at the end of Ramadan is to glimpse something of the unique quality of a city that is at the center of holiness for three major religions.

Although Jerusalem feels like a provincial town compared to Tel Aviv, it is in its religious aspects a sophisticated world metropolis that accepts in its stride the homage of the nations and, within its walls, a tremendous diversity of spiritual expression. A visitor may pass a self-proclaimed Messiah riding a donkey or come upon the formal procession of a Christian Patriarch led by heralds wearing fezzes and banging the pavement rhythmically with staves to announce the passage of the dignitary. Two millennia ago, Herod built stairways as much as 65 meters wide at the foot of the Temple Mount in order to provide the masses of pilgrims ready access. The infrastructure of the modern city is likewise designed to serve pilgrims, offering everything from spartan hospices to luxury hotels.

There is a quality to Jerusalem that makes even a non-believer feel like a pilgrim. The city receives more than a million foreign visitors a year. The bulk are divided between Christians and Jews. About 200,000 are Moslem, including many from countries that are nominally in a state of war with Israel.

Souvenir shops in the Middle Ages would sell Christian pilgrims clay flasks containing 'holy water' from the Jordan. Modern tourist shops market the same commodity in glass or plastic vials. The one place where ecumenism is indeed pronounced is the souvenir shops, where Jewish, Moslem and Christian kitsch are peddled with equal enthusiasm.

It was the Jews who infused Jerusalem with religiosity 3000 years ago, when David brought to it the Holy Ark and Solomon built the Temple to house it. It was the Christians who made Jerusalem the center of a world religion a millennium later as the site of Jesus' passion. It was the Moslems who affixed to it a new religious character 1300 years ago and bestowed upon it its principal architectural treasure.

Jews around the world pray in the direction of the Western Wall, that ancient remnant of the Temple complex built by Herod. Jewish tradition maintains that the divine spirit has

ותתצב (כרים) אחותו מרחוק

זה השער לה צדיקים יבואו בו

ויאמר אליהו בחרו לכם הפר

ויתן את צפרה בתו למשה

ספר

מליץ יושר

אלה הדברים נלקחים מספרים הרבה יקרים והם
עקרים · מתוק · כי מאוה · כל · יקר · ודברי שלום ·
נרור האור · אמתי ה' · ונעתקו ללשון אטכנז על ידי
המחבר בעל צאנה וראנה ה'ה החכם
הטוב החסיד מוהר'ר יעקב בלא'מ הר'ר
יצחק זלה'ה מטטפחת רבינו טעלה זיכה את
הרבים · ועתה נוסף עליהם פשטים נמים
ואתוקים רבים האותיטבים על הלב מהטפר
טפתי כהן טעל התור ואן טפר אטטה ה'בסדר וזאת
הברכה וזה טלא היה ברמטונים · וכלת הרבים תלוי
בהם מטר רבים אמני · הארן · אתיהרים כהיות
טנאלמים בזה החבור פטטים ואמאורים טארחיבן
לב · האדם · ומעוררין מותו ללאור כו ·
.לזכות מת הרבים הולא עור הטעם · מן הדפוס ע'י
האורפים · ועל ידי כהר'ר יעקב באוהר'ר יוחק סג'ל
וטטפחת ואאטפאם :

באמשטרדם

בשנת כתרם לבבי עשיתי זאת לפ'ק

ויפנשהו בהר האחים וישק לו

רכב וסוסי אש ויעל אליהו

והעורבים מביאים להם

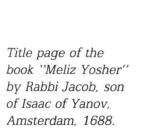

ותקח צפרה צר

בבית ובמצות

הנדיב משה קאשמן בן

הקצין וטפסר הר'ר

אליהו שלי'ט

עמרך :

ויט משה את ידו על הים

Title page of the book ''Meliz Yosher'' by Rabbi Jacob, son of Isaac of Yanov, Amsterdam, 1688.

constantly hovered over it since the destruction of the Temple itself. At almost any time of day or night, in any season, men and women can be seen praying in front of the Wall or simply standing in silence. The chinks between its stones are filled with folded notes containing prayers placed there by worshipers. Periodically, these notes are gathered up by the religious authorities, in order to make room for new ones, and buried in a nearby cemetery, which is the customary way of dispensing with old prayer books. Thousands of Jews fill the plaza in front of the Wall on Sabbath eve and on holidays. Numerous congregations pray simultaneously in this vast open-air synagogue – Iraqi, Moroccan, eastern European – and the medley of their different liturgies glancing off each other reflect the rich diversity of the Jewish exile, which began at this very spot in A.D. 70 when the Romans destroyed the Temple and put an end to the ancient Jewish state.

The diversity of the Christian presence is even more striking. There are 32 different Christian denominations in Jerusalem alone. To walk through the streets of the Old City is to be a witness to the incredible diversity of Christian worship in the Holy Land – the Greek Orthodox clergy with their pillbox headgear, the Armenians with their black hoods, the members of the Latin orders with their different colored robes, the Ethiopians, the Copts from Egypt, members of the Syrian Orthodox Church whose children are taught Aramaic, the language that Jesus spoke... The layman would be hard pressed to identify the numerous other Churches represented in the passing crowd, such as Maronites, Chaldeans and Melkites. If one were able to identify a clergyman from the Russian Orthodox Church, it would be almost impossible to tell which of two factions he belonged to – the 'Reds', who owe allegiance to church leaders in Moscow, or the 'Whites', who broke away after the Russian Revolution and now have their seat in New York.

Over the centuries, there have been conflicts among the various denominations over rights in the holy places. Clergymen have beaten, even killed, each other in the Church of the Holy Sepulcher, the holiest site in Christendom, as a result of such disputes. The Crimean War was caused, at least in part, by disputes among European powers backing different Churches in their arguments about proprietary rights in the Holy Places. For generations, the key to the Holy Sepulcher Church has been in the possession of a Moslem family, which opens the main door each morning, thus avoiding a major dispute among the Christian denominations over which should have custody of the key. Despite these rivalries, however, the various Churches maintain a vibrant religious life in Jerusalem. The high point in the Christian calendar in the city is Easter Week. On Palm Sunday, thousands of pilgrims, following the route taken by Jesus when he entered Jerusalem for his final Passover, descend the Mount of Olives towards the walled city, carrying palm fronds. On Good Friday, the pilgrims proceed along the Via Dolorosa, pausing at the Stations of the Cross. Many of the pilgrim groups collectively carry a large wooden on across their shoulders, in emulation of Jesus' agony. At night, the Church of the Holy Sepulcher is filled with pilgrims, many of them Greek women dressed in black, holding candles. On Easter morning, High Mass is celebrated in the presence of the diplomatic corps at the site marking the crucifixion.

The sanctity of Jerusalem for Islam is linked to the description in the Koran of Mohammed's miraculous nocturnal journey from Mecca to 'the far distant place of worship', Jerusalem. According to Moslem tradition, Mohammed was wakened by the angel Gabriel in Mecca and rode with him to Jerusalem on a horse with a human head. From the site of the destroyed Jewish Temple, Mohammed ascended into heaven, where the precepts of Islam were revealed to him. It is plainly the influence of Judaism and Christianity, whose combined roster of prophets and religious leaders from Abraham to Jesus was adopted by Islam, that gave Jerusalem religious significance to Mohammed and his followers in the Arabian Desert. A treasure bequeathed upon Jerusalem by the early Moslem rulers is the

Dome of the Rock, built upon the site of the Jewish Temple in 691 by Caliph Abd al-Malik. The tile-covered Islamic shrine, one of the most beautiful structures in the world, serves to this day as the architectural symbol and visual centerpiece of Jerusalem. At the southern end of the Temple Mount is the Al-Aksa (far distant) Mosque, the principal mosque in the land. Every Friday, Al-Aksa draws worshipers from around the country, as well as pilgrims from the Arab world. Five thousand can fit into the mosque's vast interior but more than ten times as many sometimes participate in the service on the esplanade outside, where the prayers are broadcast by loudspeakers.

The Temple Mount, regarded as holy by both Jews and Moslems, is the most sensitive point in the Middle East. To Islam, it is the third holiest site after Mecca and Medina. If the Western Wall at the foot of the Temple Mount is the holiest site at which Jews can pray, it is only because the Temple Mount itself is too sacred. Most rabbis forbid Jews to go onto the Temple Mount, lest they should inadvertently enter the area designated for the Temple's Holy of Holies. In that innermost chamber of the Temple, only the High Priest could enter, and then only on one day a year, Yom Kippur. Since the precise location of the destroyed Temple and its chambers is not known with certainty, these rabbis argue that Jews should stay off the Mount altogether. This ruling, initially made centuries ago, has been instrumental in preventing a head-on clash between the two religions.

In a major decision after the Six-Day War, the Israeli authorities decided to leave *de facto* control of the Temple Mount in the hands of the Moslem religious authorities. Although militant Moslems periodically stage nationalist demonstrations on the Mount and militant Jews occasionally try to pray on its periphery, arguing that the Holy of Holies must have been in the center, the stability of the area has basically been maintained and the long-running Israel-Arab political conflict has not deteriorated into an even more dangerous holy war.

Despite the tensions among the Christian denominations and between Jews and Moslems, despite the passions involved in contrasting celebrations of faith at this religious fount, a remarkable level of co-existence has been achieved on a day-to-day level. If there are miracles still to be seen in the Holy Land, none is more striking than this.

Gustave Doré: The Book of Macabees II,1–15. Angel Leading the Macabeean Soldiers.

THE INGATHERING

The refugee ships began sailing eastward from Europe even before Israel's War of Independence had ended, bringing survivors of the Holocaust to that distant shore still seething with conflict.

The newborn state had declared itself a place of refuge for Jews wherever they might be. This Ingathering of the Exiles, as it came to be known, was given priority by the Israeli government second only to the nation's physical survival. Israeli military procurement officers scouring war surplus depots in Europe for supplies for Israel's embattled army were ordered to acquire large numbers of tents for refugees at the same time.

In one of the most remarkable feats of nation-building, the 600,000 Jews living in Israel at its founding would within three and a half years absorb 690,000 immigrants, even as it engaged in a grueling war.

Since its founding half a century before, the Zionist movement had advocated limiting immigration to Palestine in order not to overburden the country's limited economic resources and create rampant unemployment that would sour the dream. Similar warnings began to be sounded in 1949, when 290,000 immigrants arrived in that single year. Health officials also warned of serious dangers of contagious diseases unless the inflow slowed down, particularly from Third World countries. However, Prime Minister Ben-Gurion ordered the gates to be kept open. Not only was there a manifest need to offer a home to the displaced Jews of Europe – even if it was only a tent for a few years – but Israel itself urgently needed to swell its numbers if it was to meet the challenges that inevitably awaited it. Within a few years, Ben-Gurion said, the problem might not be where to find work for immigrants but where to find the manpower the country needed.

The first arrivals were settled in abandoned British army camps and in Arab villages and urban neighborhoods whose previous Palestinian residents had themselves become refugees in 1948 and were now in camps in Arab countries. As these places began to fill up, tent encampments were erected near existing towns, but these too were soon filled with immigrants.

For government planners, the situation in the early 1950s presented a rare opportunity – a landscape waiting to be filled and hundreds of thousands of people eagerly waiting to fill it. A major factor in drawing up a new map was the need to raise settlements in the border areas and the empty expanses of the south, as a tripwire against armed infiltration.

These government planners, many of whom had been trained in Germany before the rise of the Nazis, had drawn up ambitious plans for population dispersal that would provide a hinterland for a country in which more than 70 percent of the population was squeezed into part of the coastal plain. The planners also wanted to lay the basis for sound regional development by creating a hierarchy of settlements from farming villages, to towns of varying sizes, to cities.

In 1951, the top official in charge of immigrant absorption visited the senior government planners in their offices. "In the past," he told them, "we settled immigrants in places where there was a town nearby with employment opportunities. Then we placed them in any abandoned houses available even if there was no employment nearby. When the pace of immigration was stepped up, we built transit camps in places where there were plans on the drawing board for building a settlement. Now I am prepared to place transit camps on sites where you're still only dreaming about a future city. Tell me the sites in your dreams and I will immediately build camps there."

To the immigrants deposited with their few belongings beside a collection of huts or tents in a patch of desert at the end of the world, the Promised Land seemed a desolate and dusty place. Within less than a decade, however, these camps would give way in a remarkable burst of creative energy to 500 new farming settlements – double the number that previously existed – and a score of new so-called development towns. This infrastructure would transform the land and its people.

In laying out this largely rural settlement grid, the planners were defying the conventional planning wisdom of the postwar era. Dozens of newly emerging nations, eager to close the gap with the industrialized world, saw their future in the smokestacks on the western horizon. Available resources were invested in new plants in urban centers, in order to draw off surplus population from rural areas.

A similar solution was urged upon Israel by foreign economic advisors who came to the country under the Marshall Plan. The Israeli planners and political leaders, however, declined to take this advice. Zionist ideology saw in the return to the soil a basic aspect of a reborn Jewish state. In addition, geo-political dictates called for a broad dispersion of settlement, rather than concentrating the population in a few urban centers.

In 1949–50 alone, 200 farming settlements were established around the country, almost ten a month. What makes this figure even more astonishing is that virtually none of the immigrant settlers had any farming experience. Veteran Israeli farmers moved into the new villages with their families as volunteers for a year or more to offer guidance and assist the agronomists and other experts provided by the settlement authorities. At the same time, an entire rural infrastructure had to be built up from scratch – from water supplies (notably, the National Water Carrier, bringing water from Lake Kinneret to the semi-arid south) to packing houses.

This was the hour of the Rural Settlement Department under the dynamic direction of Ra'anan Weitz, a young agronomist who had the vision and originality to match the greatness of the challenge. The department's policy of regional development would become a model studied to this day by planners from around the world.

Deciding against the melting-pot approach, the Settlement Department populated the new farming villages with separate ethnic groupings to reduce inter-communal frictions – the adustment to a new life was tough enough without a Yemenite housewife having to put up with the strange cooking odors from the kitchen of the Poles next door, or listen to the strange music of neighbors from Cochin, India. Thus, immigrants from Romania, Morocco, Afghanistan and Argentina in neighboring villages could live their lives in segregated, culturally cohesive communities while raising a generation of children who would share a common Israeli culture. Schools were located in regional centers, to which the surrounding villages sent their children. Here too were shops, government offices and other facilities that permitted inter-communal contact for the adult immigrants as well.

There was considerable skepticism among veteran Israeli farmers about the ability to turn immigrants with no experience in agriculture and no pioneering motivation into productive farmers. It was not easy, but within a few years refugees from the slums of Casablanca and Romanian towns were reaping what they had sown with their own hands.

Most of the farming villages were to prove an astonishing success. A survey carried

*Drawing of a bowl
ornamented with
a representation of Adam
and Eve, Poland.*

out in 1958 showed significant differences between settlements with a European population and those inhabited by people from North African or Asian countries (Iraq, Turkey,
etc.). According to ten criteria, ranging from agro-technical abilities to accounting procedures, the European villages were far stronger. When the survey was repeated in 1963,
the gap was seen to have significantly narrowed. In 1987, the survey was carried out once
more. This time, with an Israeli-born generation operating the farms, there was virtually no
measurable difference between farming villages at all.

The tent-dwellers had been transformed into a nation.

A ghost village in which nothing stirred except snakes and refuse whipped by the
desert wind greeted the immigrants descending from the trucks after the grueling ride from
Haifa in 1954. For the newcomers, there could hardly have been a more unpromising
beginning. Dressed in white cotton jackets or in saris that offered scant protection against
the winter cold, they gazed about them at the empty houses and the empty desert and the
dirt track that had led them southward past Beersheba, the last populated point on the map
of the new state.

The dream of Zion had brought 60 families of dark Jews from Cochin on the equatorial
coast of southern India to Nevatim, a forlorn desert outpost already twice abandoned by
settlers as unviable in the six years since the foundation of Israel.

Lova Eliav, the official who had undertaken to guide the Cochin Jews into this bleak land, told them that beds, food and kerosene primuses for hot water awaited them in the houses. They would get a good night's sleep and begin taming the desert in the morning.

If the site seemed inauspicious, so in truth did the new settlers. Petty tradesmen and artisans, they had no background in agriculture or hard physical labor. They had been brought to Israel only after considerable debate in Jerusalem. The medical authorities warned that members of the community suffered from elephantiasis and other exotic diseases. The threat of possible epidemic blocked the ingathering of the Cochin Jews until one of their most distinguished members, a lawyer, arrived in Jerusalem to plead their case and present medical evidence that the diseases were not contagious.

Despite lingering doubts, the authorities decided in the end that the Zionist state could not bar the gates to Jews who wished to settle in it. As a precaution, however, this group of Cochin Jews, after being processed through an immigrant station, was immediately dispatched to the most isolated settlement in the south. The word 'quarantine' hung in the air, though never uttered publicly.

Cochin Jews had been accustomed to living on the fringe of the Jewish world. According to the community's tradition, not taken overseriously by all its members, the first Jews to arrive on the Malabar coast were King Solomon's sailors searching for the spices of the East three millennia ago. There is historical evidence of the presence of a Jewish community in the area for at least 1000 years – some claim 1500 years.

Far from suffering persecution amidst a sea of Hindus, Moslems and Christians, the members of the small Jewish community were regarded as bearers of good luck and enjoyed the patronage of local princes, who granted them special privileges over the centuries. Many of the Jews were wealthy landowners, but none worked the fields themselves. The community was strongly synagogue-oriented and its youths were until recent generations educated exclusively in the synagogues. Revenue-producing enterprises like plantations were bestowed by local rulers upon the synagogues, which in turn distributed funds to the community's needy. Following the expulsion of Jews from Spain in 1492, the local community of dark Jews was augmented by co-religionists from Spain, known as white Jews, who had their own synagogues. The last century saw a serious economic decline in the community.

The Cochin Jews had kept track of the developments leading up to the creation of the

Scenes from the Esther Scroll, Germany, 17th–18th c., copperplate engraving on parchment.

65.   The outside of the Shrine of the Book 70 at the Israel Museum, Jerusalem. The white-tiled surface is built in the shape of the lid of the jars in which the Dead Sea Scrolls were found.

66.   Part of a war memorial by Israeli sculptor Dany Karavan outside Beersheba, the capital of the Negev. The memorial commemorates the Negev Brigade of the Palmach, which captured the area in the 1948 War of Independence.

67.   Students take advantage of the spring sun on a lawn within the Hebrew University campus on Mount Scopus, Jerusalem. The university was founded on this site in 1925 and now has nearly 30,000 students.

68.   Yad Vashem, Israel's central memorial to the Holocaust, comprises a Hall of Remembrance, extensive research facilities, a library and museum. The picture shows part of the Children's Memorial at Yad Vashem.

69.   The John F. Kennedy Memorial in the Judaean Hills represents a tree trunk reaching to the sky but cut off in its prime. The building was donated by Jewish communities from each of the 50 states of the USA.

70.   The promenade surrounding the Jerusalem Theater is often the site of temporary art exhibitions. This sculpture by a young Israeli artist is one such exhibit.

71. Two impressive modern buildings in Tel Aviv's business and commercial heartland. Foreground: the IBM building; behind: the Asia building.

72. The library on the campus of Israel's youngest university, the Ben Gurion University of the Negev, Beersheba. The fast-growing university has some 6000 students. One sphere in which it is especially active is arid-zone research, following the vision of Prime Minister David Ben-Gurion, the spiritual mentor after whom the university is named.

73. A lecture on Judaism for foreign students at the Mount Scopus campus of the Hebrew University, Jerusalem.

74. The Yemin Moshe quarter of
Jerusalem was the first Jewish quarter to be
built outside the Old City walls. Raised by
the British Jewish philanthropist, Sir Moses
Montefiore, beginning in 1860, it was
intended to relieve the pressure on the
thousands of Jews living in intolerably
crowded conditions in the Old City. Today it
is one of the most desirable and expensive
residential areas.

75. Yemin Moshe photographed from
Mount Zion.

76. A quiet lane in the Jewish quarter of
the Old City.

77, 79. The *tavelet* or promenade running along Tel Aviv's beachfront. Thronged with bathers and beach freaks during the day, after dark the promenade becomes a center of entertainment, open-air cafés, restaurants and ice-cream parlors until the small hours of the morning.

78. Fishermen tie up their boats for the night alongside the fishing jetty of Kibbutz Ein Gev on the eastern shore of the Sea of Galilee.

80, 81.   *The warm waters of the Gulf of
Eilat, on which lies Israel's southernmost
town, team with exotic tropical fish and
attract scuba and skin divers from all over
the world.*

82.   An aerial view of the Temple Mount, Jerusalem. On this site Abraham's hand was stayed by God from sacrificing his son Isaac. It was here that Solomon built the First Temple, destroyed by the Babylonians in 586 B. C, and Herod built the Second Temple, destroyed by the Romans in A. D. covered Dome of the Rock, often wrongly called the Mosque of Omar, since it was actually raised by Caliph Abd al-Malik in 690. The Al-Aksa Mosque, built in 710, is on the left of the Mount. The large open esplanade at the top left lies in front of the Western Wall.

83.   Many thousands of people still live in cramped conditions within the Old City walls of Jerusalem. The double-domed Church of the Holy Sepulcher lies between the Christian and Moslem quarters of the Old City.

84.   Housing in one of Jerusalem's new developing suburbs.

85.   Part of a new housing development in the Ramot quarter of West Jerusalem. The buildings are designed to provide maximum shade from the sun and privacy for each apartment dweller. The hexagonal-shaped buildings at the top are an absorption center for new immigrants.

86. The Abbey of the Dormition on Mount Zion, and adjacent roof tops. The abbey stands on the traditional site of the death of the Virgin Mary and the coenaculum, the hall of Jesus' Last Supper with the twelve apostles. The abbey is the venue today of chamber music and organ recitals.

87. The Koffler reactor in the Department of Nuclear Physics at the Weizmann Institute of Science, Rehovot. This world-renowned institute was named after the eminent chemist and long-time leader of the World Zionist Organization, Dr Chaim Weizmann, who became Israel's first president in 1948.

88, 89. The army is, of necessity, an essential part of Israeli life. Women do their full share, serving for two years (unless exempted on religious grounds), participating in all branches of the armed forces and in all spheres and functions, excepting only front-line combat troops.

90. A group of life-sized figures in grey concrete by the Israeli sculptor, Ofra Zimbalista, in a sculpture garden at the Tefen Industrial Park, Nahariya.

91.   Israelis are among the world's leading concertgoers, as attested to by this packed auditorium at Buriyanei Ha'Ooma, Jerusalem's main concert-hall. Israel has four symphony orchestras and many smaller musical and choral groups.

92.   Shopping is also very much part of the Israeli experience. The customers haggle over prices outside a popular restaurant in the heart of Jerusalem's Old City.

93.   A young man in Jerusalem's Old City market selling sahleb, a concoction made from hot milk to which has been added wild orchid, cornflour and rose water – topped with cinnamon and chopped almonds.

94, 95.   These new immigrants, patiently awaiting their turn to be 'processed' by the immigration authorities at Lod airport, are recent arrivals from the Soviet Union. It will not take them long to exchange their overcoats and fur hats for open-necked shirts and join mainstream Israelis, like those on the right, enjoying the spring sunshine at sidewalk cafés in Jerusalem's midrehov (pedestrian mall).

96.   The autumn Festival of Tabernacles
attracts thousands of Christian believers
from all over the world, who gather in
Jerusalem for five days of celebration and
song. Easter also attracts thousands of
Christians, like this Dutch choir posing on
the Mount of Olives against the background
of the Old City.

9

97.   View from the top of Tel Aviv's Hilton
Hotel, looking south toward the promontory
of Jaffa in the distance. The pool and
crossroad complex is Namir Square,
a popular center of hotels, restaurants, cafés
and places of entertainment, named after
a former mayor of Tel Aviv.

Jewish state. They had been visited by Jewish emissaries from the West, and children began to be given double first names, such as David Ben-Gurion and Golda Meir. With Israel's founding, local Zionist clubs began to exert pressure for mass emigration to Israel, and in 1949 a few young men emigrated on their own. Their subsequent letters, while hinting at difficult conditions, nevertheless urged the community to follow. The elders were reluctant to abandon the security of the income provided through the property and other resources owned by the synagogues. Their reluctance increased when emissaries from Israel made it clear that they could expect to wield hoes themselves in the new country. The young people, however, were adamant about emigration. A few families made the bold move in 1952, and a large group set out in 1954, traveling three days by train along the length of western India. In Bombay, they were provided with beds in local synagogues for two days, and then boarded a plane that carried them to Israel. This was the group that, a few days later, bedded down for their first night in Nevatim.

The site had been one of the 11 points settled on the night after Yom Kippur, 1946, to establish a foothold in the Negev. Unlike the others, it had been abandoned after the war by its initial group, to be resettled in 1952 by Holocaust survivors from Hungary and Romania. The poor soil and difficult conditions soon persuaded most of these to seek greener pastures as well. When Lova Eliav arrived to survey the moshav before the coming of the Cochin group, he found ten families still holding out. The cows they had been given, he discovered, had long since been sold on the black market in Beersheba. An air of neglect and despondency prevailed.

Eliav, who would become one of the best-known officials in Israel's settlement program, had volunteered for this, his first field assignment, after serving four years as special assistant to the chairman of the Settlement Department. He determined that the remaining European settlers must be encouraged to leave Nevatim before the arrival of the Cochin group, so that the newcomers could make a fresh start free of black-market intrigues. He did this by casually mentioning to the Europeans that they would soon be joined by new neighbors from India. "By the way, some of them aren't very healthy," he added. When the alarmed residents asked what he meant, Eliav let drop the word "elephantiasis". In a few days, the last of the residents was gone and workmen arrived to fit out the houses with beds and basic provisions for the Cochin group.

The first morning after their arrival, the Cochin Jews gathered in the moshav's storehouse, where Eliav had stocked shoes and workclothes for distribution. He had brought with him three young men who had immigrated in 1949 to serve as interpreters, since few of the new arrivals spoke anything but Malayalam, which Eliav had been told was "a minor dialect spoken by 60 million Indians". On the list he had, the newcomers were identified both by long Indian names and by Hebrew names, names like Avraham. When he called such a name, several persons would sometimes step forward and Eliav would designate them as Avraham aleph, Avrahem bet, etc.

In his first address to them the night before, when he had welcomed them to their new home and informed them about the work routine, he had noticed them shaking their head from side to side everytime his remarks were translated. Disconcerted, he asked one of his translators what they were objecting to, and was informed that such head-wagging was an indication of assent.

Handing out pitchforks, Eliav led the group out to their first task – cleaning the dirt and debris left by the previous settlers, particularly in the barns. Their first agricultural undertaking was killing the snakes, or *pampes,* as the Cochinis called them in Malayalam. The episode would still be recalled with gusto by residents of Nevatim decades later.

Shortly after the resettlement of Nevatim, Prime Minister Ben-Gurion issued a call to veteran settlements to send volunteers to help the immigrant villages springing up in their

*Detail of a fresco in
a synagogue at Dura-Europos,
Syria, 3rd c.*

hundreds across the country. Eliav was joined by three male volunteers and one beautiful female volunteer. The five formed a commune and shared the tasks of training the newcomers as farmers and educating them as citizens. The settlers had brought with them enough spices to dazzle even a King Solomon. Curries, the tearful Israeli volunteers discovered, were among the mildest.

The settlement grew to 117 families within three years as more immigrants arrived from Cochin, but its fortunes did not grow apace. Each family was provided with a sizable tract alongside its house to grow vegetables, but income came only from public works projects such as road building and tree planting. Poor soil, little water and lack of a serious agricultural background made it impossible for the breadwinners to reap a living from the soil. In a repeat of Nevatim's previous experience, families began to drift away, and by 1962 only 70 were left. In that year, however, Nevatim began to turn the corner with the return of the first small group of youngsters from the army. These youths had all attended agricultural schools and served on farming settlements during their army service. The Settlement Department allocated them land of their own at Nevatim.

The following year, the second group of young men returning from army service asked for representation on the village council. The older generation was worried that the youngsters might try to displace them on the council, but the young men said they only wanted a non-voting place so that their voice could be heard.

That voice soon became dominant. It spoke in Hebrew, while the elders still spoke in Malayalam. And it reflected a new mindset attuned to the ways and the opportunities of a new land. The passivity of the older generation gave way to a new purposefulness. At the young people's initiative, a Hebrew-speaking committee was formed to deal with the outside world.

The committee's first act was to call on the Settlement Department to halt all outside work for the villagers and focus instead on making Nevatim a viable farming cooperative. "We don't request it," they said in their meetings with the government officials, "we demand it." The young leaders said they didn't care if they went hungry for a while, but they wanted orchards planted and the chicken runs expanded. The Settlement Department, delighted at this display of initiative, was happy to comply.

Within six years, 300 acres of apricot and other orchards were planted. Taking advantage of the hot climate of the Negev, the settlement became one of the first in the country to export early fruit and vegetables to Europe, and one of the first to grow flowers for export. When they encountered initial difficulties due to the saline soil and high wind that played havoc with the greenhouses, they started again. "We were determined," one of its leaders recalled years later, "that the Cochin Jews, who they were afraid would bring epidemics to Israel, would stick it out and make the settlement, abandoned by others, a model for the country." In two decades, the export of flowers from Nevatim increased from $30,000 a year to $6 million, mostly to Holland.

Even more than an agricultural success, Nevatim has been a human success. Settlement officials point to the tact with which the younger generation eased out their elders from decision-making positions, and to the caring attitude displayed toward one another.

When new homes were built in the cooperative village, it was decided at a general assembly that the older people would get the larger houses. When inflation sent the prices of those houses spiraling, the younger generation absorbed the costs. The village also built a club where the elderly could spend the day in a variety of activities.

There are today 120 farming households in Nevatim, the largest of 15 settlements in the country inhabited by Cochin Jews. To accommodate sons returning from the army, the village council drew up plans for a suburban-type neighborhood on adjacent land so that extended families could continue living in proximity even if the younger generation pursued non-farming occupations.

The religious and folk traditions of Cochin Jewry remain a binding force in the village. Several years ago, a delegation from Nevatim traveled to Cochin, where a small number of Jews continue to live, and brought back the Torah scrolls, furnishings and wooden paneling of one of the community's beautiful synagogues no longer in use. Restored in Nevatim, it is an architectural gem which is filled each Sabbath with worshipers.

The daily cuisine at home remains largely Indian and the women still don saris for festivals. On Sabbath afternoons before weddings, the groom's friends gather at his home to sing Hebrew songs of praise for the bride composed in Cochin.

The Cochin heritage may in time provide a means of livelihood for residents not engaged in farming. There are plans to build near the settlement a tourism complex that would include a museum on Cochin Jewry, a restaurant serving Indian food, an amphitheater in which Indian dancing and singing would be presented, and a small motel.

"Twenty years ago there wasn't a single car in Nevatim, only a tractor," said one of the village leaders in 1988. "When I told friends that everyone here would someday have a beautiful home, that there would be a tractor and a car in front of every house, that there would be a village pool and a sports center, they said I was crazy. When I said we would even bring over a synagogue from Cochin, they said I was beyond help. Now look around, it's all here."

In the packing house each morning, villagers stop by to scan computer print-outs showing the prices they received in Amsterdam for the flowers airlifted from the desert settlement two days before.

In the single generation since the founders went snake hunting with pitchforks, the residents of Nevatim have not only proved their ability to enter the age of computers and modern agro-technology but have done so without abandoning the values that held the community together for more than 1000 years. If they are indeed the descendants of Solomon's sailors, they have returned from the East with something that resembles the spice of life.

Illustration of verses from the Book of Jonah, The Works of Josephus Flavius, Strasbourg, 1581.

THE MILITARY

B rig. Gen. Amira Dotan, the first Jewish woman general since Deborah made war against the Canaanites 3000 years ago, led her female troops against an even more formidable challenge than Canaanite chariots – the one posed by the image that young women have of themselves.

Promoted to command of Israel's Women's Corps, Gen. Dotan undertook in the late 1980s to shift a significant percentage of female soldiers out of conventional clerical jobs, where most pass their two years of obligatory military service, to tasks at the cutting edge of new technologies, hitherto undertaken almost exclusively by male soldiers. It was a change, she believed, that neither the army nor the young women soldiers themselves could afford to refuse.

The role of the Israeli army in peacetime has been almost as important as its role in Israel's numerous wars and in the lengthy years of border skirmishing between wars. Israel's founding fathers recognized in it a primary tool of nation-building. More than any other aspect of life, the army became the great melting pot in which veteran Israelis and immigrants from almost every country in the world got to know each other. Universal military service and annual reserve duty for men until the age of 50 was an important psychological leveling factor – the most humble of workers from an outlying development town knowing that men his age from Tel Aviv's café society were spending as much time as he – more if they were officers – on border patrol or muddy training exercises. An intimate bond inevitably develops among men from every walk of life in the same reserve unit who meet for a month every year, particularly if they have shared a war or two. Were it not for this connection, Israeli society would undoubtedly have experienced much more intense social protest from the economically deprived than it has.

The army has also been used more directly as a social instrument. In the early years, girl soldiers were sent to the hundreds of new villages around the country to help teach Hebrew and other subjects to adults as well as children. Today, the army gives high priority to a program involving marginal youth, often with criminal records – youths who in the past would not have been accepted by the army. By being drafted, the youths are spared the social stigma that applies in a society like Israel's to those who do not share the national burden. Before being assigned to regular units, these youths are given months of special education as part of their army service. The courses aim to improve basic reading skills and to induce a sense of national consciousness by teaching them something of Jewish history from the biblical period through the Holocaust to present times – a history of which they may have been aware only in vague terms. It is select girl soldiers, about the same age as the youths in this program, who serve as the teachers.

In recent years, girl soldiers have been used for much more than teaching. Following the 1973 Yom Kippur War, the need for maximalizing the army's limited manpower became evident to the military high command. This included using womanpower to better effect. Young women were given special training to serve as instructors to male soldiers in combat courses ranging from tank driving to artillery spotting, thus releasing men for combat assignments. To Gen. Dotan, the increasing emphasis in the military on technological areas opened more opportunities for her girl soldiers (aged 18 to 20). She did not, however, attempt to push for female combat roles. ''I fight for equal opportunities for male and female soldiers, but we must recognize that there are certain differences.''

Annual reserve military duty adds a curious dimension to Israeli lives. It is a burden that takes a month a year out of one's life, and in times of tension perhaps two months or more, for close to 30 years. It is physically taxing and sometimes dangerous. Although compensation is paid through national insurance for time spent on reserve duty, it is generally insufficient to cover the loss in income, particularly for people with their own businesses.

But reserve duty also has its secret joys. Foremost is the camaraderie of men accompanying each other from early manhood through middle age, exchanging familiar jokes each year as they pull on their uniforms and army boots. It is a noble excuse to escape from life's routine, from work, from one's family. (Many a wife appreciates the breathing space afforded by her husband's reserve duty as well.) It injects a sense of national purpose into one's life, a projection of the 'I' to the 'us'. It also provides an outlet for machoism that life does not usually offer men living within the confines of a well-ordered society – a government clerk charging up a hill with his infantry unit in a training exercise or an architect firing a tank cannon at a target might not admit that he's enjoying it, but he is.

Every few years, these war games would give way to war. In 1956, Israel won Sinai in a lightning strike against the Egyptian army as France and Britain attacked the Suez Canal. A few months later Israel pulled back to its borders under American pressure. The war had few political consequences but it demonstrated the fledgling Israeli army's ability to attack swiftly and to improvise in the course of battle.

The Six-Day War in 1967 dramatically changed the course of Middle East history. The Egyptians, believing that Israel was about to attack Syria, closed the Red Sea to Israeli shipping and moved their army into Sinai, where it was deployed near Israel's border. Fearing a combined attack by Egypt, Syria and Jordan, whose forces greatly outnumbered Israel's, the Israeli government hesitated for two weeks amid growing anxiety about the nation's fate. With the appointment as defense minister of Moshe Dayan, who had commanded the army in the 1956 campaign, the government approved a pre-emptive military strike.

On the morning of June 5, close to 200 warplanes, virtually the entire Israeli air force, took off from bases throughout Israel. They flew low to avoid radar detection and at precisely 7.45 a.m. the first wave struck at nine Egyptian air bases. By 10 a.m., almost the entire Egyptian air force had been destroyed and a senior officer telephoned his wife that the war was over. The war had yet to be fought – six days of bloody combat on three fronts – but the air supremacy won by Israel in those opening hours clearly dictated the outcome. Israel not only won Sinai but wrested the West Bank and East Jerusalem from Jordan and drove the Syrian army from the Golan Heights, which had dominated Israeli settlements in the north.

Coming on top of the very real fears for the physical survival of the state which had prevailed on the eve of the war, the stunning victory created a sense of national euphoria. This would last until the Yom Kippur War of 1973, when Egypt and Syria succeeded in achieving strategic surprise, sending the Israeli army reeling. Ground-to-air missiles provided by the Soviet Union caused havoc among attacking Israeli planes, and anti-tank missiles wielded by Egyptian infantry destroyed hundreds of Israeli tanks. Only after fighting a desperate blocking action to halt the Arab armies did the Israeli army manage to

Illumination from the Persian manuscript, Jami at-Tawarikh, 14th–15th c. Miniature from the 16th-c. Persian manuscript, Yusuf o Zuleikha, showing Joseph being rescued from the well into which his brothers had cast him.

turn the battle around, crossing the Suez Canal in a daring operation that changed the course of the war on the Egyptian front. On the Syrian front, the Israelis advanced to within artillery range of Damascus, despite the reinforcement of the Syrian army by Iraqi and Jordanian expeditionary forces.

This time war proved the gateway to peace, at least on the Eyptian front. Their initial successes had restored Arab pride, and in 1977 Egyptian President Anwar Sadat made his historic trip to Jerusalem. The ensuing Israel-Egypt peace agreement led to an Israeli pullout from Sinai and the beginning of diplomatic relations between Israel and Egypt.

In 1982, Israel launched an attack into Lebanon whose initial announced objective was to destroy the military infrastructure built up by the Palestine Liberation Organization in the south of the country. However, by carrying the battle up to Beirut in an attempt to impose a new political order on Lebanon, the government embroiled its forces in a battle against the strong Syrian army and protracted and bitter guerilla fighting with the numerous militias that had arisen in the political chaos of Lebanon. The one redeeming feature of the war for Israel militarily was the attack by the air force on massed Syrian ground-to-air missile batteries in the Bekaa Valley. These missile batteries, which had proven so deadly in the Yom Kippur War, were entirely eliminated without loss of a single plane after their electronic homing devices were neutralized by sophisticated counter-measures employed for the first time by the Israelis. It was not until 1985 that the army finally withdrew from Lebanon, although small detachments remained behind to buttress the Israeli-backed South Lebanese Army in the so-called security zone created by Israel as a buffer against incursions from the north. Less than three years after the Lebanon pullout, the army was called upon to deal with the Palestinian uprising.

In the relatively short span of two decades, the Israeli army had thus gained rich, if undesired, experience in dealing with a variety of conflicts ranging from all-out war on several fronts and highly sophisticated electronic warfare to suppression of a popular uprising with clubs and tear gas. Though its physical and moral reserves were severely strained in some of these efforts, the army has remained a formidable instrument of national will and even an important moral resource and unifying factor in a politically divided nation.

Printer's mark of Raphael Isaac Hayyin of Mantka, 1724–1764.

98. Tel Aviv is the center of Israel's fledgling movie industry. This wistful character was an extra in the film 'Masada', starring Peter O'Toole.

99. Two orthodox Jewish women from Peki'in. This village in Upper Galilee is the only place in Israel where Jewish residents have lived continuously ever since the fall of the Temple in A.D. 70.

100, 101. Jews, Arabs and Christians
originating from more than 80 lands
manage to coexist in Israel, each bringing
with them their own customs, languages
and beliefs. On the left is a group of Arabs
in a Jerusalem marketplace. On the right,
a Jew from Yemen in the town of Rosh
Ha'Ayn smokes a traditional nargileh or
water pipe.

102, 103.   A recent Jewish immigrant
family from Ethiopia in an absorption center
in Beersheba (left), and (right) an Ethiopian
of the Christian Coptic faith at the Church of
the Holy Sepulcher in Jerusalem.

10

104

104, 105.   A Jew from Bukhara in Soviet
Asia, and (right) a young Yemenite woman
modeling traditional Yemenite jewelry.

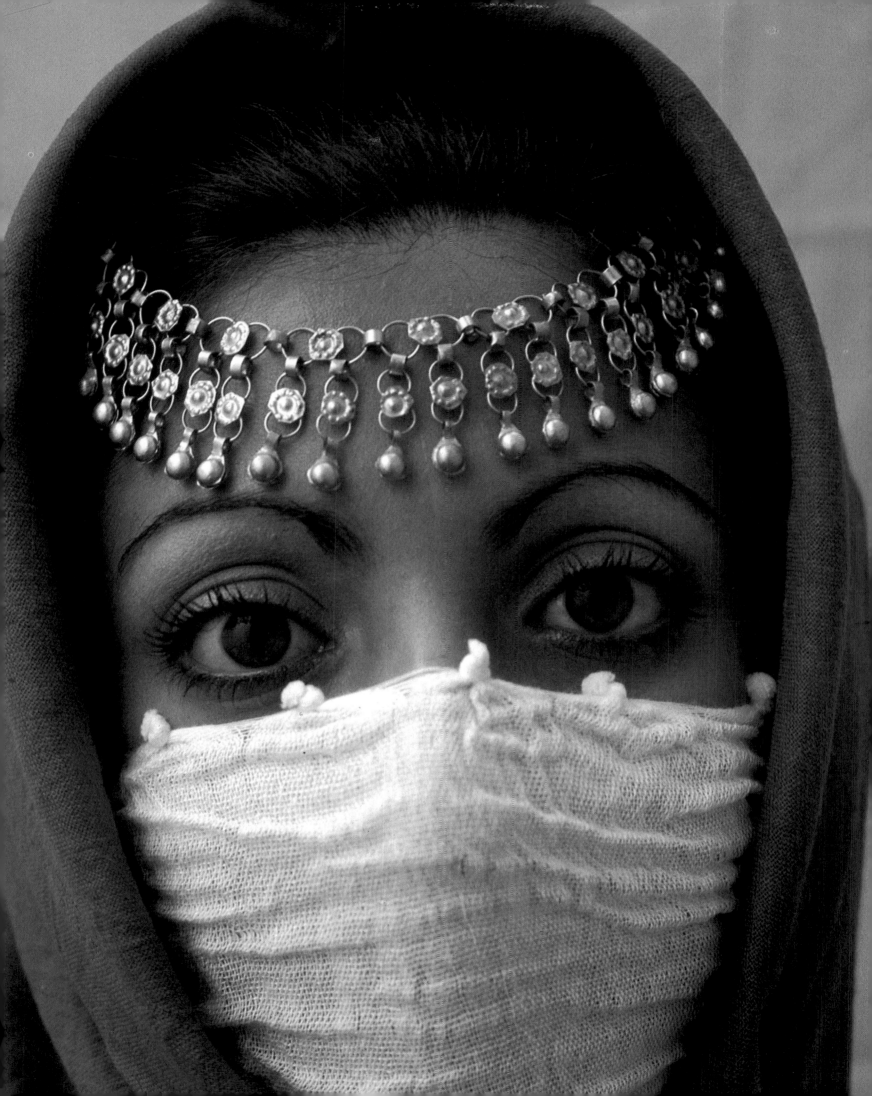

106, 107, 108. *A study in contrasts: the two men are elderly orthodox Jews: on the left, an Ashkenazi rabbi and on the right, a patriarch from Yemen. The girl in the middle needs no caption: let us just call her 'Miss Israel'.*

109. *A Sabra. People born in Israel are known as Sabras, after the local prickly pear – supposedly prickly on the outside but sweet on the inside, once you manage to get through the skin.*

THE PEOPLE

Never ask an Israeli for his life story, and certainly not his family's story, if you're in a hurry. They come from more than a hundred countries bearing tales of strange lands and shifting fortunes.

When Gen. David Lascov died in 1989 at the age of 87, he was still on active duty, the oldest serving soldier in any army. Born in Omsk, Russia, he began to study medicine – his father was a doctor – but was expelled from university because of Zionist activities. He moved to Leningrad, where he switched to architecture but stuck to his surreptitious Zionist activities. It was in the local Zionist club that he met the girl he married. Abandoning his studies, he traveled with her to Siberia with the intention of crossing into China as the first station on their way to Palestine.

The young couple was captured by Soviet border guards trying to cross the Amur River and sentenced to two months' hard labor in Siberia. Upon release, they tried again. This time they made it. Lascov spent the next few years working in construction in the Chinese city of Harbin, mostly repairs of Chinese temples. In 1928 the couple received visas to enter Palestine and sailed for Haifa. In that port city, David completed his architectural studies at the Technion and went into private practice. But life was to lead him in the opposite direction, blowing up things rather than building them.

His military career began in 1940 at the age of 38 when he joined the British army and served as an engineer. When the State of Israel was created in 1948, he joined its army despite already being 46 years old. He remained in uniform for the next 41 years, most of it as commander of a small engineering unit whose principal task was the development of special weapons. The unit's work was highly secret and three times over the years Lascov would secretly receive the coveted Israel Security Prize. A specially shaped rocket he developed – called the 'L' for Lascov – was used in the Six-Day War to destroy the Jordanian front line blockhouses in Jerusalem in the opening hours of the battle. Lascov, then a 65-year-old colonel, was himself wounded in Jerusalem after he had personally unleashed another one of his weapons in the center of the battlefield.

His mind remained so fertile that the army asked him to stay in uniform as long as he liked. He continued working until two days before his peaceful death, a long way from Omsk.

Most Israeli Jews fall within one of two categories – those of European origin, known as Ashkenazim, and Sephardim or Oriental Jews. The term Sephardi (from Sfarad, Spain in Hebrew) is more properly confined to Jews whose ancestors were expelled from Spain and Portugal in the fifteenth century – most of them settling in Italy, Greece, Holland and the Ottoman Empire – but it has come to be more broadly used in recent decades to embrace also Jews from Arab countries, whom the scholars prefer to call Oriental Jews.

Relations have often been strained between those major streams of the Jewish Diaspora, representing distinct cultures. The Zionist establishment until the state's founding was overwhelmingly Ashkenazi. The Oriental Jews who arrived in the mass immigration of the 1950s and encountered economic hardships subsequently felt themselves patronized and exploited by the Ashkenazi establishment. Periodically, resentment at the wide social, educational and economic gap would explode into demonstrations. The Likud's rise to political power in 1977 was largely fueled by Sephardi resentment at the political establishment which had been in power since 1948, even though most of the Likud leadership was also Ashkenazi.

In recent years, the gap has been perceptibly narrowed, paticularly psychologically. Ashkenazi-Sephardi differences are less a subject for protest than they were and more often a subject for mutual, good-natured, teasing – about differences in diet or the male-dominant Sephardi household, for instance. The major political parties give prominent place to Sephardi candidates in Knesset and local elections.

If the diversity of its population is one of Israel's greatest charms, integration of Sephardim and Ashkenazim is one of its greatest challenges. Although a far higher percentage of Sephardim attend university today compared with 20 years ago, it is still much smaller than the percentage of Ashkenazim who attend. One of the major forces for integration in Israel is the steady increase in intermarriage (now about 20 percent of all marriages) between Sephardim and Ashkenazim of the generation born in Israel.

Menashe Eliachar was 15 when he witnessed the surrender of Jerusalem. It was December 1917 and British shelling of Turkish positions around the city had just stopped. Making his way gingerly along the empty main street to see what was happening, the Jewish boy met a party of men including the Arab mayor of Jerusalem, Salim Effendi el Husseini, an old family friend. Some months before, the mayor and Menashe's father had made a dangerous trip across the Jordan together to buy wheat from bedouin to save Jerusalem's starving population, cut off from regular food supplies by the war. "Come with me Menashe," said the mayor to the Jewish boy, "and you'll see something you'll remember to the end of your days."

At the entrance to Jerusalem, they encountered two British sergeants who had become separated from their unit. The soldiers raised their rifles and one of the major's aides waved a white flag. To the astonishment of the wandering soldiers, the mayor delivered an elaborate surrender speech. The soldiers politely heard him out. When he was done, they pulled out cigarettes and asked if anybody had a light: they had been without matches for days, they said.

Menashe, later to become a major cigarette importer, would indeed remember the scene, and the soldiers' expression of relief as they lit up, for the rest of his life, but he would witness other events hardly less dramatic. The Eliachars were among the leading Sephardi families in Jerusalem. Their Spanish-born ancestor had arrived in Jerusalem in 1504, a decade after the expulsion of the Jews from that country. In the ensuing centuries, it was the Sephardi community that constituted the aristocracy of the Jewish population in Palestine. From among them came the leading rabbis and leading businessmen and they maintained excellent relations with their Arab neighbors. The Ashkenazi Jews from Europe were mainly elderly religious persons who had come to spend their last years praying in the Holy Land. Few of them learned to speak Arabic.

With the upsurge of the Zionist movement in Europe and the immigration of dynamic Ashkenazi youth to Palestine, this Sephardi aristocracy steadily receded in public prominence. But their rootedness and the good relations they continued to maintain with the Arab elite would remain an important resource for the Jewish community. On the eve of the months-long siege of Jewish Jerusalem in 1948, Menashe Eliachar managed to obtain a permit from the outgoing British administration for the import of a large amount of staple foods to sustain the city, emulating what his father had done in the First World War.

Menashe and his brother Eli, who would serve in the Knesset, were leaders in the mid-1940s of a movement aimed at promoting Jewish-Arab relations. The Jewish regeneration in the Holy Land, they argued, need not be at the expense of the Arabs, and the two peoples could enjoy another golden age as they had in Spain. Though this vision was overwhelmed by political realities, the Eliachars continued in the coming decades to promote the notion of Jewish-Arab friendship.

A few days after the fighting in Jerusalem ended in 1967, Menashe Eliachar was telephoned by Mayor Teddy Kollek close to midnight. No Israeli civilians were yet being permitted to enter the Arab quarters but Kollek asked Eliachar if he would go into the Old City the following morning to make contact with his old Arab friends. It was important, said the mayor, to establish communications at a personal level with the local Arab leadership. Entering the Jaffa Gate into the Old City which had been across the border of divided Jerusalem for two decades, Eliachar soon met a carpet merchant who used to work for his father. The two men embraced. So many old friends emerged to greet him that it took Eliachar two hours to make his way half a mile through the marketplace to the Arab Chamber of Commerce. There, the merchants' leaders poured out their problems. The Israeli authorities were demanding that they change their Jordanian money to Israeli money within three days and prepare an inventory of their stock for tax purposes within eight. They needed more time and they needed a more precise explanation of what was expected of them, said the merchants.

Returning to West Jerusalem, Eliachar went directly to the head of the customs department, an old friend. The man was eating a sandwich at his desk. Eliachar persuaded him to extend his deadline by a week and to come with him that afternoon to the Arab Chamber of Commerce to answer questions. He should speak in Arabic, said Eliachar, no matter how rusty it was. Eliachar then went to the director of foreign exchange in the Treasury Ministry and obtained from him as well a postponement of the exchange edict and an agreement to come to the chamber of commerce.

In the ensuing years, Eliachar and his family would maintain relations of mutual respect and affection with some of the leading Arab families in East Jerusalem. At the end of the Passover holiday each spring, during which Jews abstain from bread for a week, Arab friends would send the Eliachars trays with freshly baked Arab bread, butter and honey. The Eliachars would return the trays with delicacies.

Despite all the tensions in Arab-Jewish relationships over the years, relationships like those would sustain hope for the vision of a golden age of Arab-Jewish reconciliation.

Among the most colorful of the Oriental Jewish communities is the Yemenite. Largely isolated from the rest of world Jewry — according to tradition, for close to 3000 years — the Yemenites had developed their own distinctive culture in their remote corner of the Arabian Peninsula. In 1882, several hundred made their way to the Holy Land. They were distiguished by their wiry build, swarthy complexion, religious devotion, and clothing, which was that of Arabia. Their diligence as farm workers moved the Zionist establishment to send an emissary to Yemen in 1908 to bring hundreds to work in the new farming colonies as laborers.

Following the founding of the state, 45,000 Yemenite Jews were brought to Israel by plane in Operation Magic Carpet after they had walked across the desert from Yemen to neighboring Aden, then under British control. Fewer than 1000 were left behind in Yemen. Close to 200,000 Israelis today claim Yemenite descent. The young generation has been well integrated into Israeli society and the physical leanness of Yemenite Jews has given way as eating habits change. However, their close-knit family patterns remain, as does their work ethic, piety and pleasant disposition. Yemenite dance and song and Yemenite artisanship have been a major influence on the development of Israeli culture. Many leading Israeli singers are Yemenite.

A rich and pious Jew in Yemen indulged a century ago in the extravagant fancy of obtaining for his personal use a prayer book handwritten in Jerusalem. Since prayer books for several centuries already were being produced by printing presses, he dispatched a scribe from Yemen to the holy city with orders to write the prayer book there. The scribe is believed to have made his way on foot to Aden, embarked on a ship to Port Said at the northern end of the Suez Canal, taken the railway to Jaffa on the Palestine coast and walked up the hills to Jerusalem.

For five years, the faithful scribe remained in Jerusalem, fulfilling his mission while imbibing its air of sanctity. He used black ink made from soot and paper colored a light brown. He is believed to have worked in front of the Western Wall where scribes often sat... Many of the prayers in the book he illuminated with red-blue decorations around the script. When the scribe returned to Yemen he presented his two-volume, 750-page work to his wealthy patron. Some 60 years later, the two volumes, called the Jerusalem Tikal, would be carried back to the Holy Land by the patron's descendents in Operation Magic Carpet.

They sold it in the 1950s to a fellow Yemenite, Rabbi Yehyia Garmi, a dealer in holy books. Garmi was also cantor in his synagogue in Jerusalem and used the prayer books when leading the service. When he died, his son Shmuel inherited the books. Shmuel was praying from the Tikal on Yom Kippur in 1973 when an army courier arrived in the synagogue to announce mobilization.

A tank commander in a reserve unit, Garmi was the next day with the first battalion to climb the Golan Heights to support the thin line of regulars barely holding the Syrian army at bay. Garmi had had no time to go home from the synagogue and the Tikal rode into battle with him in his personal kit. In the first day's battle, 37 of the battalion's tanks were knocked out but Garmi's was unscathed. Slowly, reinforcements reached the front and the tide of battle turned.

Weeks later, Garmi was interviewed by a reporter visiting the muddy front where the Syrian and Israeli armies faced each other awaiting political negotiations that would permit a pullback. The short, thinly-bearded sergeant was asked how his livelihood had been

affected by his extended mobilization. "Oh," he said with seeming cheerfulness, "financially I've been ruined." Garmi had survived the fighting but his diamond-cutting business had indeed been ruined by his absence. To restore his fortunes, he moved with his family after the war to Belgium, where he became a diamond merchant. Within a decade, he had earned enough to return to Israel to do what he really wanted to do – publish Yemenite Jewish holy books. His first effort was a facsimile reproduction of the Tikal his father had given him.

At the other end of the cultural spectrum from the Yemenites are the *yekkes*, as immigrants from Germany are called. The yekke is characterized by fastidiousness and punctuality. German immigrants were prominent in setting up the country's educational and law systems, although many early idealists, sometimes with medical or other degrees, became pioneers who worked the land. Following the rise of the Nazis, Jews from Germany and Austria provided the first substantial middle-class immigration, bringing capital that was invested in businesses and fledgling industry. They also brought standards of cleanliness and order which they fought mightily to impose on their new Levant surroundings. The haggling of the oriental bazaar had no place in a yekke emporium. Immigrant German Jewish musicians made up the majority of players in the new Israel Philharmonic Orchestra, which gave its first concert under the baton of Arturo Toscanini in 1936. German Jews also came to constitute a high percentage of doctors and other professionals in the land.

Richard Kaufman won an Iron Cross in the First World War fighting with the Kaiser's army on the Western Front. He was wounded at Verdun when he led a group of comrades trapped in a valley through the French lines to safety. Born in Frankfurt to an assimilated Jewish family, he had hoped to be an artist, but studied architecture and town planning when his father insisted he learn a profession. He was soon embarked on a meteoric career, interrupted by the war, and won several prizes. In 1920, he left it all behind when he received a letter from a Zionist settlement official in Palestine asking him to design the new communal settlements that were beginning to be established in large numbers.

Immediately after arriving in Jerusalem, he traveled to the Jordan Valley to visit the first kibbutz, Degania. He found it to be "a prefect example of incorrect planning". The dining hall and dwellings were downwind from the garbage dump and barn, he noted. In the next 38 years, he would virtually shape the countryside in the Jewish areas, designing 120 kibbutzim and moshavim. He drew up innovative designs as well for 'garden' neighborhoods in Jerusalem and other cities which are still highly desirable residential areas. He also designed buildings, introducing a Bauhaus style architecture stressing function. The villa he built for an Egyptian Jewish banker in Jerusalem is today the official residence of Israel's prime minister.

His primary joy, however, remained the design of rural settlements for the new Jewish farming class. "While the farmer in North or South America is happiest when from his doorway he can not see his neighbor's chimney," he wrote, "the Jewish farmer wants to live close to his colleagues. His need for personal contact and conversation, and especially his high cultural needs – for lectures, discussions, music, theater, reading, chess – obliges the builder to place in the center of each settlement, large or small, a cultural hall." Another special need of the new settlements was security, which meant choosing a site that dominated its immediate surroundings and making at least one building stout enough to serve as a redoubt in case of attack.

His admiration for the pioneers affected his own lifestyle. Although he loved company and earned quite well from his prolific labors, there was only the barest of furniture in his Jerusalem home, and little food: he did not wish to become a bourgeois materialist. Though he had a wife and two daughters to support, he gave much of his money away. If a new

*Scenes from the
Esther Scroll, Germany,
17th–18th c., copperplate
engraving on parchment.*

kibbutz urgently needed a cow, for instance, Kaufman might buy it one. Sparsely furnished as his home was, it was often filled with settlers engaged in passionate discussion on how their ideals of equality and cooperation could best be expressed in the physical design of their kibbutz or moshav.

"I don't know of any place in the world," wrote Kaufman, "that can offer as much satisfaction to an architect and planner as this country. Here we are beginning from the beginning."

One does not have to be born in Germany to be a yekke. Prof. Joshua Prawer was born into a well-to-do merchant family in Bendzin, Poland, close to the German border, and grew up in a central European cultural environment. In addition to Polish, he spoke German on the streets, and studied Latin and Hebrew, in both of which he became fluent. Yiddish, the vernacular of most Polish and Russian Jewry, he did not learn until he joined the Zionist movement, when it proved useful for communication with Jews from other regions. His fluency would also extend to French, English and other languages. He arrived in Palestine in 1936 on his own at the age of 19 to study at the Hebrew University. His first thought was to study mathematics, but he soon discovered to his suprise that the level of the Palestinian Jewish students in the subject was higher than his own. At the suggestion of his father, who wired him, he switched to history.

His mother died before the outbreak of war in Europe and his father and the rest of his family disappeared in the Holocaust. Joshua planned to leave the university to join a kibbutz but was dissuaded by his teachers. With support no longer available from his family, he maintained himself by newspaper delivery and other odd jobs. Casting about for a subject for his thesis, he conferred with his professor. "You have a European education and you're going to stay on here," said the professor, "so let's find something that connects the two." The subject they settled on was the Crusades.

It was a field Prof. Prawer would make his own, becoming one of the foremost authorities in the world in the coming decades. He approached the subject differently from his colleagues abroad, viewing the Crusades not from the perspective of Europe but from the perspective of the Holy Land itself, analyzing the life and thought of the Crusaders during the 200 years they dwelt on its shores. The Crusades were a favorite historical analogy for Israel's enemies, who saw the Jewish state as an outside imposition that would likewise disappear. The Crusaders, however, had constituted only a small fraction of the population and were technologically backward with respect to the Moslem world. Jews today constitute 83 percent of Israel's population and the country is in terms of military technology one of the world's leaders. One basic difference was that the Crusader knights had come to lord it over the land, which was farmed only by Arabs, while Israelis had come to settle the land and work it.

Of the 1.4 million immigrants who arrived in Israel until 1971, the country that provided the most was Morocco (253,000). The strong family and communal ties of Moroccan Jews was severely tested by the realities of the new land. The second generation, however, began producing genuine leaders, particularly in the small but rapidly growing 'development towns' where many of the new immigrants had been deposited after their arrival during the great immigration wave of the 1950s.

Meir Shitrit was seven when he arrived in Israel with his family from a small village near Fez in Morocco. They were settled in Yavne, a town in the south of the country. In antiquity, it had been the home of one of the great academies of Jewish learning, but there was little of distinction to mark the seedy town in which Meir grew up. Neither of his parents was literate and as the youngest of nine children, Meir's future did not seem particularly promising. But despite his parents' inability to help him with his studies, and the difficulty of finding a quiet corner at home in which to study, Meir did very well in school. He skipped two grades and, in the absence of a local high school, went to a boarding school in the center of the country for his secondary studies. There he came into contact with children from other backgrounds. Too young when he graduated to enter the army, he enrolled in university as a biology student.

His contact with the world outside Yavne impressed upon Meir that another way of living was possible. Meir's older friends expressed the same sentiment when they came on leave from the army. Sitting together during weekends, they decided that the neglect and lethargy which gripped their home town was no longer acceptable. They organized a public committee and chose Meir as its chairman, although he was a year or two younger than the others. The group organized public meetings where they found general support for their demand for youth clubs, better education, improved municipal services Half of Yavne's 10,000 residents turned out for a rally called by Meir to demand improvements. When this failed to move the local town council to action, Meir organized a massive sit-down on the main road passing through Yavne that tied up traffic for an hour and a half. The next day he began his army service.

Meir completed an officer's course and in the 1973 Yom Kippur War served as operations officer of a medical battalion on the Egyptian front. At war's end, he returned to Yavne to head a reform list challenging the entrenched political leadership in town. He had been tempted to heed his superior officer's request that he stay on in the army but decided that grass-roots reform in development towns like Yavne was more important. Ten of the town's young men had been killed in the war so the campaign was kept low-key. Nevertheless, the reform list outperformed all the others, and on February 1, 1974, Meir Shitrit, 25, sat down behind the mayor's desk in Town Hall.

Mayor Shitrit vigorously wielded the new broom he had promised against cronyism and slackness. Inefficient municipal employees were fired. New hiring practices were introduced and administrative procedures were reorganized to ensure closer supervision. Meir gave his new department heads considerable independence but demanded results. He

Purim ball at the Music Academy in New York, 1865.

went to court to stop illegal building even when the builder was a personal friend. When prospective residents threatened to break into a new block of flats whose completion the Housing Ministry was unaccountably delaying, the mayor sent a wire to the ministry saying that he would join the takeover unless the ministry moved promptly. A week later, the apartments were completed.

The young mayor met with neighborhood committees to encourage them to paint rundown buildings, plant greenery around the houses and keep their area clean. He urged parents to keep their children in school, comparing the short-term advantages they gained from sending their children to work at an early age with the long-term advantage of education, and citing as examples himself and other local youths who had gone on to university. He pushed through the construction by the government in Yavne of the kind of housing that would attract new Russian immigrants with high education and former Yavneites who had attended university. In his early years as mayor, while still a bachelor, he himself lived in his parents' house, sharing a tiny room with a nephew.

Slowly, he could feel the town shifting direction. The exodus of young people after army service slowed down and new people began moving in as housing and factories were built.

"The human material here is marvelous," said the mayor. "Despite the lack of development and cultural facilities, it is a population that is alive and vibrant. They're willing to do a lot if they're given the hope that things will improve. Yavne is a giant wheel full of rust. If I manage to give it the push that will start it turning, the problem will then be how to stop it, so that the town doesn't grow too big or too quickly. But I want to give it that push." Men like Meir Shitrit have done much to narrow the gap between Sephardi and Ashkenazi and inject a new dynamism into Israeli society.

The clearest measure of the diversity of the Jewish population is in the profusion of synagogues. Jerusalem alone has some 800 serving 350,000 Jews. Not only does every ethnic and national grouping have its own synagogues — often with distinctive decor, customs and even liturgy — but each of these larger groups breaks down into more intimate congregations, sometimes linked to a specific village or region in the 'old country', sometimes linked to some shared level of piety or liturgical leaning. For anyone interested in how the Jewish people adjusted their religious practices during 2000 years of wandering while adhering to the central tenets of their faith, the synagogues of Israel hold an endless fascination.

The black-clad ultra-orthodox Jewish sect had for long been regarded as an anachronistic marginal phenomenon of the Israeli mainstream. In recent years, those margins have measurably widened, creating turbulences as they project into the flow of secular life about them.

Called *haredim* (God-fearers), the ultra-orthodox are the fastest growing population group in Israel. Eight to nine children per family is an average. Although generally referred to as Hassidim, only about half are actualy members of Hassidic sects, that is, followers of charismatic *rebbes*, who are regarded as intermediaries between man and God. The remainder, while pursuing the same path of piety, are oriented to the scholarly world of the *yeshivot*, or talmudic academies.

As their numbers increase, the haredim have become ever more forceful in their demands regarding religious legislation, exercising their growing power both through mass demonstrations and through their representatives in the Knesset (Israel's parliament), where the haredi vote, about ten percent of the total, often represents the critical balance between the two major political blocs. These issues range from legislation that would ban public entertainment or transportation on the Sabbath to more esoteric questions such as conversion practices.

Although they seem cast from a single mold, the haredim in fact constitute an even more bewildering kaleidescope of factions than the rest of Israeli society put together. What is astonishing is that a way of life that is such an apparent throwback to the Middle Ages should prove so vital and regenerative.

The origins of Hassidism lie in eastern Europe more than 200 years ago, when charismatic personalities emerged in poor and downtrodden Jewish communities to preach a new approach to religion, a gospel of joy and emotional immersion in prayer. It was an approach that had mass appeal but was severely condemned by learned rabbis of the time, who regarded the focus on the personality of the rebbe and the ecstatic nature of Hassidim as idolatrous. The way to God, they argued, lay not in ecstatic prayer but in study of Holy

מגדל עוז שם יי

בו ירוץ צדיק ונשגב

Printer's mark of the well-known printer Gershom Soncino, 15th–16th c.

Writ. The rabbis sometimes issued excommunication orders against the Hassidim in an attempt to stem the tide but they could not. In time both groups, the Hassidim and the *Mitnagdim* (opponents – that is, opponents of Hassidim) learned to live alongside each other in relative peace.

In the past century, both groups suffered severe inroads from the impact of modern society, which drew many young men from their ranks. These breakaways and their children played an ever more prominent role in the secular life around them in Russia and Poland as secular scholars, businessmen, revolutionaries, and professionals. Some became pioneers in Palestine. The Holocaust seemed to be a final blow as the heart of ultra-orthdox Jewry in eastern Europe was destroyed.

The postwar revival of ultra-orthodoxy in the West has been astonishing – the haredim themselves, understandably, call it a miracle. Nowhere has this revival been more strong than in Israel, where some 50,000 youths are enrolled in yeshivot – far more than had existed in eastern Europe before the war. The Hassidic world has likewise revived, focussed on those leaders who had made their way to the West before the war or who managed to survive the Holocaust.

To visit a Hassidic 'court' late on a Friday night in Jerusalem's Mea Shearim quarter or the Tel Aviv suburb of Bnai Brak is to step back a century or two into the ultra-orthodox world of eastern Europe. The Hassidim join the rebbe at his *tish* or table for his Sabbath meal. The tish is not in the rebbe's home but in a synagogue which can accommodate the hundreds who come. Sometimes, grandstands are arranged around the table, at which sit the rebbe and elders of the community, so that the younger men and students, dressed in their Sabbath robes, can watch the proceedings. In between courses, there is a rousing singing of Hassidic songs, the young members on the grandstands swaying back and forth in unison. Some Hassidic leaders have seen in song a greater expression of piety than prayer, and many of the Hassidic groups have their own composers who set religious passages to music. At some point during the tish, there will be a hush as the rebbe delivers *ah vurt,* a word, that is, a brief talk on some learned subject.

One of the rebbe's most important functions is to make himself available to his followers – indeed, to anyone – for guidance. A Hassid will make no significant decision

Eduard Moyse, Circumcision, 18th-c. copperplate engraving.

before consulting with his rebbe, whether it be establishing a business, moving house, marrying off a child or undergoing an operation. The rebbe will receive petitioners late into the night, offering advice and serving as an important psychological anchor.

Traditionally, the haredi world has distanced itself from secular Zionism. The revival of a Jewish state was a Messianic promise to be fulfilled by divine intervention, as they saw it, not a political act. Many haredim, indeed, regarded the establishment of the state as an act of impiety. To this day, there are extreme haredi elements in Israel that refuse to accept Israeli citizenship and denounce the state as a desecration. Most haredim, however, have come to accept the state, some even seeing its creation as a step towards divine redemption. The bulk of haredi youth are exempt from full military service by virtue of being theology students, a point that evokes deep resentment among the rest of the population. Although some join the army reserves after completing their yeshiva education in their mid-20s, it is almost always in support rather than combat units. Haredi leaders argue that it was the ultra-orthodox who through the centuries kept the fires of Judaism lit, a function no less important than guarding the frontiers today. While not all secular Israelis altogether dismiss this view, what dismays most of them about the burgeoning strength of the haredim, in addition to military deferment, is the removal of a substantial section of the population from 'productive' labor and its periodic attempt to impose part of its worldview on the society around it.

The ranks of the haredim have been swelled in recent years by members of the Oriental Jewish community, mainly of Moroccan and Iraqi background, who have adopted the dress and customs of the eastern Europeans. In addition, a good number of 'born-again' Jews, including immigrants from the U.S. and other western countries, have shifted from a secular life, even hippiedom, to ultra-orthodoxy. This trend is not all one-way. A constant outflow from haredi ranks has enriched Israeli society with a range of talented figures, from novelists to generals. There have been periods, even in the recent past, when there was a net outflow from the haredi camp, and the cyclical nature of life makes it likely that it will happen again. Meanwhile, the haredim constitute a growing force that Israeli society must learn to live with.

In the summer of 1973, Motti Ashkenazi, a doctoral student at the Hebrew University, sat in a downtown Jerusalem café talking politics with a friend. Egyptian President Anwar Sadat had the day before offered to reopen the Suez Canal if Israel staged a partial withdrawal from Sinai. Unless Israel soon opened a dialogue with Egypt, Ashkenazi said, war was inevitable.

A few months later, Captain Motti Ashkenazi, on his stint of annual reserve duty, took command of the northernmost fortification of the Bar-Lev Line along the canal. On one of his first patrols, he found footprints on the shore behind the lines suggesting an Egyptian reconnaissance patrol. The night before Yom Kippur, he and his men could hear tanks taking up positions opposite them. Ashkenazi knew that the war he had predicted was almost upon them.

The attack was launched the next day. In the bitter fight that ensued, every one of the strongpoints along the canal fell except Ashkenazi's, which held out until relieved. Ashkenazi would remain mobilized for another four months. Two days after returning to civilian life, he showed up opposite the office of Prime Minister Golda Meir in Jerusalem's government center carrying a placard. ''Grandma – your defense minister is a failure and 3000 of your grandchildren are dead.'' It was a rainy day and people passing in buses cast no more than a curious glance at the solitary figure. The next day other demobilized reservists joined him. Ashkenazi came every day and every day the crowd with him grew larger, demanding the resignation of the government, and particularly of Defense Minister Moshe Dayan. A few months later Golda Meir resigned, taking the government with her.

The friend with whom Ashkenazi had discussed politics that summer day in 1973 had been killed in the war. Ashkenazi himself became a manufacturer of children's toys and flirted with the idea of a political career. This eluded him, but he had secured for himself a footnote in history more sizable than most politicians ever achieve – the lone protestor who was instrumental in bringing down a government and who helped implant in Israel's consciousness the notion of political accountability.

Israel's 700,000 Arabs constitute 15 percent of the population, but their impact on the texture of life in Israel is both smaller and greater than that figure implies. The tensions remaining from Israel's War of Independence, along with the country's ongoing confrontation with the Arab world, and in particular with the militant Palestinian organizations abroad, has kept the Arab sector at the margins of mainstream Israeli life. Nevertheless, they occupy a place near the center of the national consciousness. Aspects of Arabic culture like language, food and customs of hospitality have influenced the general Israeli culture, and the Arab village with its dominant minaret is a distinctive part of the Israeli landscape.

Except for the interval of the Crusades, Moslems had ruled the land since the seventh century. Israel's War of Independence in 1948 turned them virtually overnight from a majority in the land into a small minority. Of the estimated 750,000 Arabs living in the territory that became Israel on the eve of the war, only some 150,000 remained behind in their homes when the fighting ended. Most of the others were living in refugee camps in surrounding countries.

The transition from enmity to shared citizenship in the new state was not easy. Until 1965, Arab areas remained under the control of a military government rather than the civilian organs of the state. The natural sympathies of Israel's Arabs with their brethren abroad led the Israeli authorities to free them from the requirement of army service in order to avoid the strains of dual loyalty.

Nevertheless, the life of Israeli Arabs has been transformed since the founding of the state. Electricity and water lines were laid to the country's Arab villages, almost totally bereft of a modern infrastructure. Compulsory education for girls was introduced in the Arab sector for the first time, and many Arab young men and women went on to Israeli universities. The markedly improved educationdal level, particularly among women, is the main reason for the halving of the birth rate in the Arab sector, which had been among the highest in the world, averaging eight or nine children per woman. At the same time, the standard of living among Israeli Arabs has risen dramatically. Traditionally a rural society based heavily on agriculture, the Israeli Arab sector has seen a steady inflow of villagers to Nazareth and other Arab urban centers in recent decades. About 150,000 now live in Arab cities or mixed Arab-Jewish cities.

The removal in 1967 of the border separating Israel from the West Bank with its Palestinian population revived the identity crisis among Israeli Arabs, who had begun to acclimatize themselves to the Israeli reality and to live relatively easily with the notion of being both Israeli and Arab. They were confronted by a West Bank Arab society which plainly lagged behind the material and educational advances made by Israeli Arabs, a society that even looked alien to younger Israeli Arabs. As the years passed, however, the Israeli Arabs found increasing identity with Palestinians living beyond Israel's borders and became increasingly distressed by their own ambivalent position between these two worlds. That same position, however, may confer upon them in time a critical role as a bridge between these worlds.

Diplomats are accustomed to portraying their government's unpopular positions as if they were brilliant examples of logic and reasonableness that must be plain to any unbiased observer. But the new Israeli consul-general taking up his post in Atlanta, Georgia, undoubtedly realized that he might have special problems in explaining Jerusalem's

Scenes from the Esther Scroll, Germany, 17th–18th c., copperplate engraving on parchment.

positions regarding the Arab question. Consul Mohammed Massarwi was himself an Arab, the first ever appointed by Israel to a diplomatic post.

"I am both an Arab and an Israeli," he said on the eve of his departure for the United States in 1987. "We of the younger generation of Israeli Arabs have been demanding opportunities for full integration into all aspects of Israeli life. I see my appointment in the foreign service as just such an opportunity."

The 47-year-old lawyer from a Galilee village made no secret of his favoring the creation of a Palestinian entity alongside Israel, a position contrary to that of the government which approved his appointment. But this difference was something he could live with if the government could. "I feel myself to be part of a very broad Israeli consensus on the striving for peace with the Arab world. There is no sure-fire prescription for how best to attain that peace."

One of his brothers, an engineer, was already living in the U. S. where he had married a Jewish woman, also Israeli born. They had two children, one of them being raised as a Moslem, the other as a Jew. One of the first diplomatic missions the consul set for himself was to persuade them to return to Israel.

A prominent minority group in Israel is the Druze, an Arabic-speaking sect which split off from Islam in the Middle Ages. Dwelling in a score of villages in Galilee and on Mount Carmel and numbering 75,000, the Druze way of life is similar to that in the Arab villages around them, but they are set apart by their distinctive dress, religion and political attitudes. They had linked their fate to the Jews during Israel's War of Independence and proudly serve today in the army and border police.

About 15 percent of the Arab population is Christian, constituting the bulk of the more than 100,000 Christians living in Israel. They are concentrated in the city of Nazareth and villages in the Galilee Hills as well as Jerusalem. Over the years, the Christian proportion of the population of Israel and the West Bank has steadily dwindled, both because Arab Christians have a markedly lower birth rate than Arab Moslems and because many Christians emigrate to the West. In 1967, for instance, 18 percent of Jerusalem's Arab population was Christian; two decades later the figure was ten percent.

Thousands of foreign Christian clergy reside in the country, serving in the Holy Places and charitable institutions, living a life of contemplation in monasteries and convents, and

studying. For most, it is a life dedicated to spiritual pursuits well removed from the turbulent currents of secular life around them. Some, however, choose to step out of this cloistered world to partake of the life of modern Israel.

Father Marcel Dubois was not just a priest, he was a Dominican, the order which had instituted the Inquisition and led the persecution of Spanish Jews. His appointment in 1980 as head of the philosophy department of the Hebrew University in Jerusalem was therefore a rich historical irony, appreciated by none more than Father Dubois himself. "Imagine the paradox, a son of the Inquisition teaching Christian philosophy to Jewish students at a Hebrew univesity."

During the Second World War, he had been a novice priest at a Dominican seminary outside Paris that gave shelter to a large number of Jews, despite the risk. This sense of shared destiny with the Jews touched a strong chord in him and he later came to Israel to study Jewish medieval philosophy at the Hebrew University. The French priest formally joined his fate with Israel when he acquired Israeli citizenship, receiving it at his request on Christmas Day. "We don't want to live among Jews but with Jews, and we can only live with them here as Israeli citizens." He was invited to give lectures at the Hebrew University on Christian philosophers and Aristotle and was eventually appointed chairman of the department. He is, he believes, part ot the vanguard of the Church's historic reconciliation with the Jewish people.

Israel's annexation in 1967 of East Jerusalem, including the historic Old City, brought within its boundaries the most important holy sites in Christendom and a host of Christian congregations which had established themselves over the centuries in proximity to the sites in and around the city.

The Eastern Churches predominate, the Greek Orthodox being the most ancient and largest ecclasiastical body in the Holy Land. A Greek-speaking Christian community existed in Jerusalem as early as the second century. Although the Church's congregation is today almost entirely made up of Christian Arabs, the upper ranks of the Church hierarchy consists entirely of priests of Greek origin.

The Armenian Church in Jerusalem is almost as old. The Armenian Quarter, within the walls of a monastery, is virtually a self-contained village. Here live not only Armenian clergy but a secular population made up of descendents of Armenians who fled the massacres in Turkey during the First World War. These secular Armenians work in the city as jewelers and tile-makers and at other traditional crafts. They are provided housing in the monastery rent-free but must be inside before the gates are shut in the evening. Inside the compound are secular facilities, including schools, a printing press, a library and club rooms. The community maintains close contacts with the Armenian Diaspora and with Soviet Armenia.

The Latin (Roman Catholic) Church struck roots in 1099 when the Crusaders captured Jerusalem and established the Latin Patriarchate. The final defeat of the Crusaders two centuries later saw the retreat of the Western Church as well, but the Patriarchate was restored in the nineteenth century as western influence began to be felt on the Ottoman Empire. The Latin community today has more than 40 religious orders and congregations in the Holy Land. It includes many hundreds of clerics and well over 1000 nuns belonging to 26 congregations. Although the number of local members is relatively small, the Church's institutional presence is a massive one. Within the Holy Land there are no less than 170 Roman Catholic churches and chapels, a third of which are Holy Places, and close to 200 educational and charitable establishments, including schools, orphanages, clinics and hospitals, seminaries, and research institutions.

Rosh Ha-Shanah (New Year), woodcut, 1508.

Each large church community is granted by the state a large measure of autonomy in

matters of personal status, such as marriage, divorce, alimony and confirmation of wills. In other civil matters, jurisdiction is conditional upon the consent of the parties involved.

Since the mid-nineteenth century, Protestants have maintained a presence in the Holy Land. Missionary work among Jews and Moslems was the intention of the early groups, but most of their converts came from the ranks of the Greek Orthodox. The Anglicans, Lutherans and other Protestant Churches maintain schools, hospices and hospitals.

Immigrants from English-speaking countries were relatively rare until after the Six-Day War, when Israel, infused with a new dynamism, began to draw western Jews in sizable numbers. Edward Peretz arrived in 1968 at the age of 47 with a successful career as a specialized farmer behind him, hoping to put his knowledge at Israel's disposal.

Peretz bore a well-known name – his great-uncle-had been one of the most famous Yiddish writers in Europe – but he himself knew virtually nothing about Judaism. Born in England to immigrants from Poland, he had spent more than 20 years in the Channel Islands and New Zealand growing tomatoes in glasshouses. Enrolling with his wife in a Hebrew language course in Jerusalem, he began to put out feelers to Israeli agricultural officials about the creation of a glasshouse tomato industry. Israel's climatic and soil conditions made it more suitable for this purpose than any other country he had ever been in, he said. The profusion of sunny days and relative absence of frost meant that glasshouses could be built without the expensive heating facilities needed in places like Jersey and New Zealand. Tomatoes grown in glasshouses could soon surpass citrus fruit as Israel's prime agricultural export, he claimed. Initial reactions were negative. Glasshouse-growing of tomatoes, he was told, was economically unfeasible in Israel.

Peretz kept plugging until he found an official interested in his proposal. So interested, in fact, that the official pulled out a map and asked Peretz to pick the spot where he wished to set up an experimental greenhouse. Peretz did not know the country well enough to choose, but every weekend he traveled to a different region in a car driven by the official's aide. One Saturday, as they drove past fields in the Western Negev, Peretz suddenly asked the driver to stop. In what seemed a sandy waste, healthy-looking crops were growing. They were being watered by sprinklers, and the absence of puddles told Peretz the soil was well drained, a major requirement in glasshouse growing. The land was flat, which meant that it would be easy to build glasshouses. The next day, when he checked meteorological records, he found that there was virtually no danger of frost in the area. He had found his site.

By the next growing season, Peretz and his wife were living in the neighboring moshav ready to start farming in their new glasshouse. The tomato variety they selected was a kind which was being grown in open fields at four tons per quarter-acre, of which one ton was export quality. In two seasons, Peretz averaged 20 tons per quarter-acre, of which 16 tons were export quality.

The agricultural authorities decided to create an entire moshav based on glasshouse-growing of tomatoes, with Peretz as instructor. He laid down one condition – he would choose the families who would settle there. Since he had never mastered Hebrew, he preferred settlers from English-speaking countries, to whom he could give instruction easily. Accompanied by a settlement official, he traveled to Jewish communities in the U. S. and elsewhere looking for "healthy people with good backs, high intelligence and a positive attitude towards life". Hundreds of candidates expressed interest and after a lengthy selection process several dozen were chosen, all of them college graduates and most of them professionals. Within two years, they were raising tomatoes in the Holy Land, one more minor miracle for Israel.

110. Israel is a leading exponent of growing vegetables and fruit under long plastic covers. The resultant 'greenhouse effect' allows cultivation of off-season products for the winter markets of Europe and the USA.

111. A major cash crop is cotton. Israel exports both raw cotton and cotton products. The bulk of Israel's precious water resources is used in agriculture – as in these early-morning sprinklers – and farmers must be careful not to exceed their quotas.

112. Israeli agriculture is highly mechanized and sophisticated, so as to reap the maximum yields from its limited land and water resources. Israeli agricultural experts have served as advisors in dozens of Asian and African nations since the early 1950s.

113. Arab farming in Israel traditionally clings to the hillsides. Olive trees in Samaria provide high-grade oil for human consumption and for use in the manufacture of soap and toiletries.

114. Every centimeter of the hillside is exploited by the careful use of stone terracing. Some of these terraces may be hundreds of years old.

115.   Herons at Kibbutz Ma'agan Michael
on the Mediterranean coast. Israel is on the
major migratory route of hundreds of
species of birds who leave Europe in the fall
for Africa's warmer climes and return in the
spring. They can be a hazard both for
aviation in the area and for the dozens of
fish ponds, which provide uninvited free
meals for the voracious visitors.

116.   The Hula Valley in the shadow of
snow-capped Mount Hermon, Israel's
highest point. These kibbutzim lie on land
reclaimed when malarial Hula Lake was
drained in the early 1950s.

117.   The Galilean Valley of Jezreel – the
Emek as it is known in Israel – is one of the
most fertile parts of the country. It is
referred to in the Bible as the Valley of
Esdraelon.

118, 119. *A slightly newer form of communal agricultural settlement than the kibbutz is the moshav, where each family owns its own house and farms its own land, but shares in marketing and planning, the use of agricultural equipment and in social and community affairs. One of the most famous moshavim in Israel is Nahalal, which was designed on the principle of the radiating spokes of the wheel. On this moshav, the famous Israeli soldier and statesman, Moshe Dayan, was brought up, and was buried.*

120. These olive trees and the ancient
terracing on which they stand lie below
Jerusalem's Old City walls.

120

121–124. Kibbutzim have become almost synonymous with Israeli society. The first was founded by the shores of the Sea of Galilee in 1909, on the basis of an egalitarian social commune living and working together on the soil. Today, less than three percent of the population live in the 280 kibbutzim, but they wield an influence far in excess of their numbers, with a heavily disproportionate share of ministers, Knesset members, army officers, senior civil servants, etc.

125. These fishermen are laying their nets at dawn along the upper reaches of the Jordan River.

THE KIBBUTZ

Early this century thousands of Jewish young men and women from the universities and ghettos of eastern Europe made their way across the Mediterranean to Palestine with the intention of becoming farmers. Quixotic, mad or visionary, theirs was an act of breathtaking daring – an attempt not only to redeem an ailing land but to redeem, through themselves, an ailing people cut off from its roots.

Farming had been the Jews' principal occupation in antiquity, but since their exile they had lost this primal connection with the soil. They had become traders, artisans, bankers, shopkeepers. Barred by law or circumstance in most countries from owning land, they had become accustomed over the centuries to their role as rootless middlemen. The young pioneers who arrived in Palestine were determined to change this by recreating a Jewish peasant class as the base for a healthy and productive nation. In the words of a song they sang, "We have come to the Land to build and to be built."

Much of the land available was malarial. Following the expulsion of the Crusaders in the thirteenth century, the Moslems had destroyed all the coastal cities to deny Europe a foothold if it should ever attempt to launch a new Crusade. In the process, the water systems, including acqueducts had deteriorated, leaving much of the coastal plain swampy.

Jewish farming colonies had already been established at the end of the nineteenth century under the patronage of Baron Edmond de Rothschild, who subsidized them and, in effect, ran them through his agents. A new dynamism was unleashed in 1909 when a small group of pioneers established the first kibbutz, or collective, at Degania on the shores of Lake Kinneret. The kibbutz concept was an exercise in pure idealism. All property would belong to the commune, down to the clothing the members wore. There would be complete equality among its men and women members, and decisions would be taken by majority vote. There would be no hired labor, so as not to exploit others. Despite malaria, woeful ignorance of farming, and often strained personal relationships within the stultifying confines of a small group, the kibbutz survived. The first baby born a Degania was Moshe Dayan, later to achieve fame as one of Israel's foremost military leaders. Within five years of Degania's founding, there were a dozen other kibbutzim.

A major turning point occurred in 1920 when a large tract of land in the Jezreel Valley, some 12,000 acres, was purchased by the Zionist movement from a landowner in Beirut. Instead of continuing with the small Degania-style model of kibbutz, the settlement leaders decided to build large collectives on this ample tract which could profit from economy of scale and engage in small industry and crafts as well as agriculture. The large kibbutz also permitted educational, cultural and sports activities denied the small commune. The Jezreel Valley model would soon be emulated with great success around the country.

The kibbutz movement, with its fount of idealism, became the spearhead of the

Zionist movement in Palestine. As land was acquired, the Zionist leadership planted scores of new kibbutzim to create a new geo-political map. Often these were 'tower and stockade' settlements, thrown up overnight with a protective fence and watchtower already in place by dawn, in case of attack. Many of the Jewish community's leaders, such as future prime minister Golda Meir, came from kibbutzim, and it was the sturdy young kibbutz farmers who provided the backbone of the underground military force, the Haganah. By the time of the founding of the state in 1948, kibbutzim constituted 149 out of the 291 Jewish villages in the country.

Since the creation of the state, the role of the kibbutz has declined in relative importance, but it still carries weight in Israeli society far beyond what demography would dictate. Although only three percent of the country's population, its members constitute 30 percent of air force pilots and a similar or higher percentage of other elite military units. There are likewise twice as many kibbutz members in the Knesset as is warranted by proportional representation. Kibbutzim account for a percentage of the country's agricultural production well beyond their size, and six percent of its industrial exports. Even though kibbutz members all draw the same amount of pocket money each month, no matter how hard they work or what job they do – a situation the would ordinarily discourage initiative or diligence – their productivity is far higher than that of salaried workers in the general economy.

The kibbutz, perhaps Israel's most distinctive feature, has changed its nature as it

Rosh Ha-Shanah (New Year), illustration from the Minhagim (Book of Customs), woodcut, Amsterdam, 1723.

adapts to modern life. The establishment of the state deprived the kibbutz of its critical role at the cutting edge of the national movement The majority of its members were no longer idealists who had made a conscious decision to join, but people who were born into the commune. The monk-like asceticism of the early kibbutzim in material matters has gradually given way to suburban-style comforts as they seek, amid ongoing debate, to somehow blend the communal ideal with the individualistic demands of human nature.

A basic change affects the Children's House, the traditional kibbutz system in which children grew up not in their parents' home but in a separate house together with children of their own age. Looked after by a housemother, they visited their parents every afternoon but slept and ate with their own peer group. This system was aimed at affording children equality in their upbringing, while at the same time freeing the parents for productive work. But in the past two decades, an increasing number of kibbutzim have relented under the pressure of mothers who insisted on raising their children in their own homes. By general consent, however, when children reach high-school age, even in these kibbutzim, they exchange the parental home for a communal house shared by their classmates.

The emphasis on equal treatment means that even kibbutz members who are government ministers take their turn on the duty roster to work in the kitchen of the communal dining hall and spend occasional Saturdays in the orchards picking fruit. Key roles in the kibbutz have been traditionally rotated, so that someone who was the commune's top executive one year might be assigned to the cow shed the following year.

Lighting candles for the feast of Hanukkah, illustration from the Minhagim, woodcut, Amsterdam, 1723.

However, the principle of equality is being severely tested by the greater specialization demanded as the kibbutz turns increasingly to industry, now generating more than half of kibbutz income, and adopts modern agro-technology. It has proved difficult to prevent the emergence of a managerial class which, while nominally equal, has built-in privileges such as an office car and occasional business trips abroad.

Likewise, the ideal of communality has inevitably been eroded by technology and greater emphasis on individuality. Until recently, for instance, there were no telephones in members' apartments (kibbutznikim, as they are called, are not *residents* of a kibbutz but *members*). The idea was to discourage members from isolating themselves within their own four walls and promote instead the notion of an extended family by having everyone come down to the communal dining hall or kibbutz office to make and receive calls. For the same reason, kitchens were initially not built in kibbutz apartments and television sets were confined to the communal social hall. This idealism has retreated headlong in recent years before demands for a less spartan lifestyle. Most kibbutz apartments now have telephones, television sets and small but handsome kitchens. Even the hitherto sacrosanct Saturday night communal meeting, which all members were expected to attend in order to make decisions on kibbutz affairs, is now broadcast in some kibbutzim on cable television to members who prefer to stay at home and watch it passively.

A major problem has been to persuade youngsters to return to the commune after completing their army service rather than pursue careers in the cities. Instead of being

The Search for Hamez, a custom connected with the Passover (Pesah), illustration from the Minhagim, woodcut, Amsterdam, 1723.

fitted into a job slot immediately upon being demobilized, young people are permitted to take a year or more off to travel and get the wanderlust out of their system. At any given moment, kibbutz youngsters with backpacks can be found trekking through the Far East or South America. The kibbutzim have also become very liberal in permitting those who so choose to attend university or receive special training – such decisions are made at the weekly communal meeting. In the past, permission was generally restricted to those who wished to study subjects that could be useful to the kibbutz, such as agriculture or engineering, but now it is increasingly given even for studies such as art history, in order to accommodate the desires of the younger generation. In recent years, about 50 percent of kibbutz youth have chosen to stay on.

Despite the strains, despite the seeming anachronism of idealistic communal oases in the midst of an acquisitive society, the country's 280 kibbutzim remain a dynamic force in Israeli society. They have shown that they have the flexibility to bend with the times while retaining their basic vision of social equality, the dignity of labor and service to the nation.

They were 100 young men and women, all 19 or 20 years old, working as hired hands for the farmers in Gedera, one of the southernmost Jewish villages in Palestine. It was 1946 and the group was one of many *garinim*, or settlement nuclei, which had been distributed among veteran farming villages in order to receive training that would prepare them to found a kibbutz of their own.

Shortly before Yom Kippur, the holiest day in the Jewish calendar, the group was

Blessing of the New Moon, illustration from the Minhagim, woodcut, Amsterdam, 1723.

summoned to a meeting. Their leader announced that the moment they had been training for during the past two years had arrived. The group had been chosen along with ten other garinim to participate in a major settlement enterprise. The Zionist leadership had decided to stake a claim to the Negev, which constituted 60 percent of the country's land mass but was virtually empty. The British Mandatory authorities would not permit settlement there so as not to antagonize the Arabs, The operation would therefore have to be carried out surreptitiously. Under a Turkish law which still still applied in the country, a structure could not be demolished or its occupants evicted if the building was already roofed. By the time British troops arrived at the settlements, if all went well, the roofs would be up.

The operation was planned for the night that Yom Kippur ended. The British, said the leader, would not expect activity of this kind at the end of a fast day. The kibbutz they would establish would be called B'eeri. Only 25 men and five women would participate in the operation because of the sparse resources available. The remainder would join after the kibbutz was on an economically sound basis

The Haganah, in charge of logistics, prepared pre-fab huts for the 11 settlements and organized 200 trucks to carry supplies, including water.

Rina was one of the girls chosen for the B'eeri group. She was a wireless operator and her skill would be needed. The group's jumping-off point was a kibbutz to the south. They set off on foot from there with an armed Haganah escort at 3 a.m. At dawn, their guides led them up a hillock surrounded by wooden stakes marking the settlement boundaries. Around them in the growing light they could see an undulating desert emerging, totally

Purim – a Jewish festival, illustration from the Minhagim, woodcut, Amsterdam, 1723.

barren except for a clump of trees in the distance. Near the trees was a bedouin encampment.

Clouds of dust marked the approach of the trucks bearing the huts and equipment. The desert chill was soon forgotten as the settlers and the Haganah escort pitched in to set up the camp. By noon, three huts were standing on the hilltop along with a tin-walled shower stall and an outhouse. As soon as the last nail was hammered in, the men and women began dancing a circular hora and singing. The Haganah men then wished the settlers well and took their leave.

During the next year and a half, the settlers devoted their energies to fortifying the site with trenches and bunkers and to building a water pipeline to the nearest point with wells. On the eve of the British departure from Palestine, in May 1948, British tanks rolled up to B'eeri and smashed through the front gate. The commander's message was an expression of concern. The British would no longer be able to protect the settlers, he said, and with Arab armies preparing to invade, the settlers would be slaughtered if they did not pull out. Similar warnings were being delivered to the other Negev settlements. The settlers repaired the fences and dug deeper.

The Egyptian army crossed the border on May 15 with tanks and artillery and began attacking the settlements in their path. In B'eeri, Rina followed the progress of the battles on her radio, including the final words of the radiomen in settlements about to fall. The worst news she kept to herself, not wishing to add to the burden of her 29 colleagues.

On July 15, the battle reached their closest neighbor. Backed by air attacks and tanks, the Egyptians broke into the settlement but were driven out by a counterattack.

Now it was B'eeri's turn. From their positions in the trenches, the defenders could see the Egyptians crossing the terrain towards them. The settlement came under heavy shelling. Two kilometers from the kibbutz, the Egyptians halted to sever the water line and then turned away. The Egyptian command had decided to expend no more efforts on the isolated settlements which had already diverted them from their drive towards Tel Aviv – diverted them sufficently, it would develop, to permit the Israeli army to muster its forces and drive them back across the border.

The B'eeri settlers would live for ten months in underground bunkers on a diet consisting almost exclusively of tinned sardines, yellow cheese and biscuits. At war's end, none of the structures erected on the first day was still standing. But unlike some of the other ten settlements established with them, they had suffered no casualties. Abandoning the trench-scarred hill, they began again on a new site two kilometers away, where the rest of their garin joined them. Now at last they could begin to battle against the desert.

In the ensuing years, the bleak, dusty landscape turned an incredible green as the kibbutzim began to work the land. In the settlements themselves, simple huts gave way to handsome housing linked by tree-lined paths. Forty years after the state's establishment, B'eeri numbered 800 members and half of its 100 founders were still there. The settlement was surrounded by lush fruit orchards, and cotton and wheat fields, as well as cow sheds and chicken runs. But half the kibbutz's income came now from a modern printing plant, which had won a national prize for efficiency.

One winter evening after telling the tale of the kibbutz's founding to a visitor, Rina stood inside the entrance to the modern dining hall as rain lashed the lawn outside and beautiful children, some of them her own grandchildren, dashed gleefully in and out of the wet. The bulletin board in the lobby announced forthcoming cultural activities. The evidence of resounding success was all around her, but Rina was restrained in her summing up. Of B'eeri's youngsters returning from the army, she noted, many more were asking to go to university than the kibbutz had allowed for. "It was easier for us," she said. "We had the equality of poverty. No one had anything."

Rina's generation had been part of an heroic age. They had been confronted by adversity and risen to the challenge. Their children and grandchildren have been left to define their own challenges. "None of us imagined that the desert would flourish as it does today," she says. "The question now is the future of the kibbutz."

Israel's agricultural achievements constitute an amazing success story. A land that was largely desert and could barely sustain its small population a century ago with primitive farming is now a world model for agricultural development, exporting some $2 billion in farm produce annually. The average annual growth rate of agricultural production since the founding of the state has been seven percent, mostly through technological innovations. Squeezing the last drops out of its meager water resources, Israel has brought life to desert land never before farmed. This land produces winter vegetables, and even flowers, for Europe — flowers valued at $1 million were exported in 1968, as against $150 million 20 years later. Only four percent of the population in today involved in agriculture, compared to 25 percent in the 1950s, but they produce so much that 40 percent of agricultural production value is exported.

One of Israel's most far-reaching agricultural innovations is drip irrigation, wherein a mix of water and fertilizer is fed directly to the roots of the individual plants through plastic pipes, in contrast to sprinkler irrigation, which is wasteful of water. Drip irrigation has been adopted in numerous countries around the world, including Arab nations.

The country's agricultural research centers are constantly devising new technologies that keep Israel at the forefront of world agriculture despite its severe limitations in land and water. Each year some 600 people from 60 countries come to study Israel's farming methods, while Israeli experts in turn serve as advisors abroad.

Most farmers live in cooperative villages known as moshavim. Unlike the kibbutz, the moshav is made up of individual farmsteads but operates as a cooperative in purchasing, marketing, use of heavy machinery and other aspects. These villages, mostly settled by new immigrants with no farming background, became a major vehicle for Israel's phenomenal growth in agricultural productivity. However, as agriculture becomes ever more sophisticated and specialized, the moshav system, which allocates the same amount of land, water and credit to all, has come to be seen as anachronistic. New forms of villages permitting greater individual enterprise for more efficient farmers and providing non-agricultural employment for others are being proposed in their stead as Israel looks towards the year 2000.

Scene from the Esther Scroll, Germany, 17th–18th c., copperplate engraving on parchment.

THE COMMON HERITAGE

History in the Holy Land is not a dry tale embalmed in books. It is a story still being pieced together on the basis of new evidence dug up by archeologists. Over the past century, history has been unearthed from Israel's soil with increasing frequency – vivid, untold chunks of history, glittering with secrets waiting to be deciphered.

The number of full-time archeologists employed in Israel, some 200, is greater than in any other country in proportion to the population, and perhaps in absolute terms as well. They are joined each year by foreign archeological teams in a massive search for a heritage that belongs not just to Israel but to the world.

The first biblical archeologist can be said to have been the Byzantine empress, Helena, whose son Constantine in the fourth century adopted Christianity as the official religion of the Roman Empire. Helena traveled from Constantinople to Jerusalem in order to identify the holy sites described in the New Testament. Gathering testimony from local Christians to whom the early traditions had been passed down, she identified the location where Christ had been crucified as well as numerous other places associated with the biblical story. Her son, the emperor, erected the first Christian shrines upon these sites.

Helena was also attributed with the discovery of pieces of wood belonging to the True Cross upon which Jesus had been crucified, though scholars would remain skeptical about the authenticity of this and other 'true crosses' that appeared over the centuries.

An authentic link to the New Testament story is the stone inscription uncovered in 1961 beneath the sands of Caesarea bearing the name of the Roman procurator, Pontius Pilate, who had ruled in Judaea from A.D. 26–36 and who had sentenced Jesus to death. The capital of the Roman province of Judaea had been the coastal town of Caesarea, not far-away Jerusalem.

Another recent find more indirectly echoing the New Testament story was a bent nail which turned up in a small stone sarcophagus containing the bones of a man who had died in Jerusalem about the time of Jesus. The sarcophagus, with the name Yehohanan inscribed on it, was among a number unearthed when a bulldozer digging foundations for a house in Jerusalem exposed a 2000-year-old tomb. Archeologists found that one of Yehohanan's heel bones had a nail driven through it. Although crucifixion was widely practiced in the ancient world, this was, remarkably, the first archeological evidence of it ever discovered. After crucified persons died, the nails were pulled out before the victim was buried, but in this case the nail had bent against a knot in the wood and could not be extricated. What made this find especially resonant was that it had been made only two miles from the traditional site of Jesus' crucifixion, and that Yehohanan had lived and died at roughly the same time as Jesus.

A fishing boat which had sailed the Sea of Galilee (Lake Kinneret) about the time of Jesus was found buried in – and preserved by – mud when the waters of the lake receded during a drought in 1986. There was nothing to link it directly to the New Testament account of Jesus and his disciples, but the vessel was clearly similar to those that they had sailed in. The eight-meter-long craft was found in remarkably good condition but was endangered by exposure to air. It was floated to a neighboring kibbutz where it was submerged in a specially-built pool filled with a heated chemical mixture for a seven-year-long bath that would ensure its preservation.

Although the biblical period has naturally been the focus of attention in Holy Land archeology, it represents only a thousand-year swathe, albeit an especially rich one, in a tale going back more than a million years. The Ubediya site south of Lake Kinneret may in time become a national park marking this first known staging area for early man emerging from Africa on his way to conquer the earth. Numerous sites in the country trace the development of man down through the long Stone Age through his discovery of metals and agriculture, long before the biblical period.

The transition of the indigenous population from a pastoral to a settled people can be seen at Tel Yarmut, a little-known site in the Judaean foothills. The city is mentioned in the Bible as one of the confederation of five city-states that tried to halt the invading Israelites under Joshua at Gibeon. Two thousand years before that, however, about 3200 B.C., the first settlement had been founded on the site. All through the region, tribes that had been herding sheep and goats on the desert fringes, as did the Patriarchs, were beginning to settle in fixed locations and turning to agriculture. It was a Mediterranean agriculture based on vine, olive, wheat and vegetables. These settlements would establish in good measure the human geography of the biblical landscape.

Within a few hundred years of the establishment of the first settlements – in Yarmut's case, less than 300 years – these open villages would give way to walled cities. It is evident that as men accumulated wealth, they learned too the art of war. Yarmut was one of the largest of these early Canaanite cities, covering some 40 acres. The builders of its first walls, with no previous experience, experimented boldly with engineering principles. Massive stones, some more than three meters long and weighing several tons, were quarried and stacked upon each other. The builders quickly adopted the header and stretcher principle, placing stones alternately perpendicular and parallel to the line of the wall in order to bind them better.

One of the basic design principles of fortified cities was adopted by those first builders – laying out the ramp approaching the city gate so that any arrival, presumably carrying a shield in his left hand, exposed his vulnerable right side to the guards on the wall. Atop the wall, the planners built battle platforms from which the defenders could launch arrows and spears.

Impressive signs of central planning also mark the internal layout of Yarmut. Houses were grouped in small clusters with their own paved streets, an intimate pattern favored by many planners today. Pottery-making and other manufacturing activites were kept together in a lower part of the city, downwind of the residential quarters, where they would not constitute an ecological nuisance. The site was abandoned after 1000 years for reasons that are not clear, and reoccupied during the biblical period. Even before its reoccupation, however, it may have figured in the biblical story. Archeologists believe that the remains of ancient Yarmut, or a city very like it, may have been seen by the dozen Israelites sent by Moses to spy out the land. Returning to the tribes awaiting them in the desert, they reported a land of milk and honey, but one occupied by giants. "We were in our own sight as grasshoppers," warned ten of the scouts who argued against entering the land. "They are stronger than we." Archeologists have found no evidence that a race of large men ever inhabited the land, but the report of giants, they believe, may have been based on sightings of the huge stones used at Yarmut and other abandoned cities that were already ancient in biblical times. The scouts may have assumed that only a race of giants could have built on such a massive scale.

One of the central problems that biblical archeologists have focussed on for more than half a century, and still have not resolved, is whether the biblical description of the conquest of Canaan by the Israelites under Joshua should be taken as an accurate historical account. For a long time, leading American and Israeli scholars argued on the basis of archeological evidence that it should. However, a school of thought led by German scholars maintained that the biblical account, written centuries after the event, was too simplistic. In reality, they argued, there had been a slow and peaceful infiltration of Israelite pastoral tribes into the country from across the Jordan River. Only when Israelite strength had increased over the course of several generations were there military clashes leading to final Israelite rule, according to this view.

Seeming confirmation of the 'literal' school came at the large Galilee site of Hazor, which figures in the biblical account of the conquest. Archeologists there uncovered evidence of a massive fire that destroyed the city in the twelfth century B.C., when the Israelite period began. After that destruction, the site had been settled by people with a relatively primitive material culture. This was seen as clear support for the biblical account, which specifically speaks of Hazor's destruction by fire. The poor material culture of the subsequent settlers would neatly fit the situation of the Israelites emerging from desert wandering. But there was much evidence to the contrary. At many of the sites which the Bible says Joshua captured, for instance, archeologists found that no city had existed at the time of the Israelite incursion. An increasing number of scholars in recent years have come to favor the peaceful-infiltration theory, leaving room for military confrontations towards the end of this period.

A biblical event for which there is powerful documentary corroboration is the capture of the Judaean city of Lachish by the Assyrians in 701 B.C. as they marched on Jerusalem.

Hanukkah lamp, used for the festival of lights commemorating the purification of the Temple in 165 B.C., bronze, Italy, 15th c.

The supporting evidence comes not from the Holy Land itself but from far-off Iraq, site of ancient Assyria. There in the ruins of Ninevah, a British diplomat-archeologist in the nineteenth century unearthed the palace of Sennacherib, the king whose capture of Lachish and siege of Jerusalem is recounted in the Old Testament. Largely intact in the debris was a series of large stone reliefs depicting the siege and capture of Lachish and the departure into captivity of the survivors. Plainly based on sketches made at the scene by a combat artist, the reliefs offer us the only picture we have of how the ancient Israelites dressed, their weaponry, their oxcart transportation and of some of the household goods they took with them into captivity. A cuneiform inscription accompanying a relief portraying the king reads: "Sennacherib, King of the Universe, King of Assyria, sat upon a throne and viewed the booty taken from the city of Lachish." The scene echoes the biblical description of the event: "Sennacherib, King of Assyria, came up against all the fenced cities of Judah and took them."

Excavations at Lachish have identified the precise spot on which the artist must have stood to make his sketch – today a chicken coop of a moshav. They also revealed remains of the siege ramp, depicted in the relief, on which the Assyrian battering rams stood as they broke down the city walls, as well as numerous arrow heads and stone sling-shots. It is the oldest siege ramp ever found.

Sennacherib failed to take Jerusalem – the Israelite king, Hezekiah, supported by the prophet Isaiah, withstanding the Assyrian siege. But little more than a century later a Babylonian army under Nebuchadnezzar succeeded in capturing the Israelite capital. On the way, the Babylonians also captured Lachish, which had meanwhile regained its vitality since the Assyrian invasion. In the guardhouse at the main gate to the city from this period, archeologists found a score of letters written in Hebrew on potsherds. One of the letters offers poignant evidence of the mounting tension at the approach of the Babylonian army. Apparently written by an officer in an outpost tracking the signal fires maintained by the Israelite settlements in the area, it said: "We are watching for the signals of Lachish . . . for we cannot see Azekah." The city of Azekah, also mentioned in the biblical account, had apparently fallen.

Little had been known about the Philistines, apart from the biblical account, until recent archeological excavations. It is clear from these digs that the modern use of the term Philistine as an epithet meaning an uncultured boor does a gross injustice to the ancient Philistines, who had a highly developed culture. Their early pottery shows the clear influence of the Aegean culture from which they stemmed. At the Philistine site of Ekron, archeologists have made the biggest oil strike Israel has known: more than 100 olive oil installations, including presses and other facilities needed for oil production. In antiquity, olive oil played at least as large a role as petroleum does today, being used for lamps, medicines and much else. Located in a well-defined 'industrial zone' at the edge of the city, the ancient oil production area at Ekron is the largest ever found in the Middle East.

Probably the most sensational archeological find in the Holy Land during the past century was the cache of ancient documents known as the Dead Sea Scrolls. They were found not by an archeologist but by a bedouin shepherd boy, who in 1947 discovered jars inside a cave into which one of his goats had wandered. Inside the jars were large rolls of parchment covered with writing. The documents were brought to an Arab antiquities dealer in Bethlehem and then shown to a Hebrew University archeology professor for evaluation. The astonished professor found himself reading an original Hebrew text written 2000 years before. The desert climate in the cave alongside the Dead Sea had preserved the documents so well that they were easily legible – the biblical-style Hebrew could indeed be understood by any Israeli schoolboy. Subsequent searches in the caves in the area uncovered numerous other documents.

Floor mosaic of Hammath synagogue near Gader (El Hammeh), Transjordan, 15th c.

213

It soon became apparent that these cave documents were linked to the nearby remains of a settlement at Qumran. As scholars reconstructed it, the settlement had been founded in the second century B.C. by an ascetic Jewish sect known as the Essenes. Cutting themselves off from mainstream Judaism of the period, the Essenes lived a monastic life at Qumran under the initial leadership of a man known from the documents as The Teacher of Righteousness. One of the rooms in the settlement had been a scriptorium, in which holy books and other works were written. The Essenes are known to have had a strong influence on early Christianity. In A.D. 70, as the Roman army marched down the Jordan Valley to Jerusalem, the inhabitants of Qumran hid the parchment documents from their extensive library in the nearby caves, wrapping them in linen and placing them in covered jars for safekeeping. Although the Essenes apparently hoped to return to their settlement at war's end, Qumran was never reoccupied and the scrolls were to remain hidden for 2000 years. Many of them are today on exhibition at the Israel Museum in Jerusalem.

One of the most popular archeological sites for tourists is Massada, a half hour's drive along the Dead Sea from Qumran. The mountaintop fortress where the Israelites made their last stand against the Romans in A.D. 73 has been partially restored since its excavation in the 1960s, and a cable car provides a quick ascent. The view from atop Massada of the Dead Sea and the Mountains of Moab is as dramatic as the site's history.

After 1967, the major archeological site in the country became Jerusalem. There were suprisingly few ancient remains visible in the city before then, the sanctity of Jerusalem and its built-up nature having discouraged extensive excavation. The Israeli authorities, however, made the unearthing of ancient Jerusalem a major national priority once access was gained after the Six-Day War to the sites on which biblical remains might be buried. As some officials put it, it was an attempt to dig up Israel's title deed to the land by exposing its ancient roots. However, in digging up their own roots, the Israeli archeologists also exposed the extensive Moslem and Christian roots in the land and, to their credit, they restored and preserved these as carefully as the Jewish antiquities.

Three massive excavations were launched in and adjacent to the walled Old City. A normal archeological digging season is generally from a few weeks to two months, the rest of the year being devoted to recording the finds, analyzing them and preparing for the next year's dig. However, one of the Old City digs went on for up to nine years without a break, and the others were almost as epic.

Digging at the foot of the Temple Mount on a site that had been used to pasture goats, one of the three expeditions cut through 26 layers of civilization, reflecting the sweep of peoples and cultures, from the Persians to the Crusaders, who were drawn over the millennia to Jerusalem, despite its remoteness from the main routes of antiquity. Each civilization built on the ruins of the one it had destroyed or otherwise displaced, making use where it could of the old foundations and rebuilding with the old stone blocks in its own style. As the Crusaders put it: "A castle half destroyed is half built."

Of all the layers exposed, the most impressive by far was that of the Second Temple period, 2000 years ago, when the city was more populous than it had ever been or would be again until this generation. It was the heart of world Jewry, which numbered about six million, including those scattered throughout the Roman Empire, where they constituted some ten percent of the population, as well as those living beyond the imperial borders. Three times a year, there was a mass pilgrimage to Jerusalem. King Herod, who ascended the throne in 37 B.C., undertook a vast building program to enable the city to cope with an inflow of as many as 100,000 pilgrims on these occasions — a number not much less than the city's permanent population of 150,000. He doubled the size of the Temple Mount and provided it with massive flights of steps, as much as 65 meters wide, on its main approaches, built scores of ritual baths to enable pilgrims to immerse themselves before entering the holy precinct, laid out broad paved streets lined by shops, and set aside areas for hostels and campsites. To provide water for this large influx of pilgrims he constructed a sophisticated drainage system to capture a maximum amount of rainwater in reservoirs.

Jerusalem was in this period the focus of enormous spiritual ferment. Schools of religious learning proliferated and mystical sects like the Essenes were preparing for the coming of the Messiah. This is the city in which Jesus walked and where he died. Until the archeological excavations which began in 1968, virtually the only physical remnant of this period was the massive support wall surrounding the Temple Mount platform. The most famous section of this support wall, known as the Western Wall because it was located on the western side of the Mount, became for Jews over the centuries a proxy for the destroyed Temple itself. The utilitarian support wall thus became imbued with a sanctity far beyond its original prosaic function. Beneath the surface of the surrounding terrain, archeologists found many architectural fragments from the Temple complex which had been thrown off the Mount by Roman soldiers in the frenzy of destruction, including pillars from the Royal Portico, described by the historian Josephus as being so thick that it took three men with outstretched arms to encircle one. When the broken pillars were uncovered, archeologists found Josephus' description to be accurate.

A large Moslem palace whose remains were unearthed at the foot of the Temple Mount proved one of the most suprising finds – the surprise being that even Islamic historians were unaware that a royal palace had been built in Jerusalem shortly after the Moslem conquest. From the roof of the lavish palace, a short bridge had permitted the caliph to walk directly into the Al-Aksa Mosque on the Temple Mount. The palace courtyard had gardens fed by water channels, and orange trees suffused the courtyard with a sweet scent. Adjacent to the palace were auxiliary buildings, including large baths. For 1200 years this impressive Islamic complex had been lost to history until uncovered and preserved by a Hebrew University expedition.

Hanukkah lamp, Italy, 16th c.

The second major Jerusalem archeological dig was in the Jewish Quarter of the Old City. This had been the elite neighborhood during the Second Temple period, home to the senior priests and aristocracy. It was ironically the devastation of war that permitted this archeological probe. Many of the buildings in the quarter had to be demolished because of damage inflicted in the 1948 war, as well as the ravages of time and neglect. The authorities decided that as buidings were demolished, archeologists would be permitted to excavate the site before new buildings were erected.

What they found were the remains of fabulous mansions larger and better appointed than virtually any villa in modern Jerusalem – including one measuring 600 square meters on each of its two floors. These had sunken baths and beautiful mosaic bathroom floors, elegant stucco-ornamented walls and ceilings, and brightly-colored murals reminiscent of the contemporary city of Pompeii. Much of the wealth evident in these structures had been left behind by the hundreds of thousands of pilgrims each year who paid a Temple tax, beside spending an abundance of shekels with local merchants.

The dig also uncovered grim evidence of the last hours of this glorious period: soot-blackened rooms attesting to the fire that consumed the quarter when the Roman soldiers broke through the last defenses and wreaked their vengeance on the city and its inhabit-ants. In one basement room, archeologists found a spear in the corner which its owner had not managed to reach. On the threshold of a kitchen was the skeletal forearm of a woman who had tried to flee.

The Jewish Quarter dig also uncovered major Christian structures of the Byzantine and Crusader eras, particularly one of the most magnificent churches of antiquity, the sixth-century Nea Church. Built by Emperor Justinian and vividly described by contemporary historians, the 116-meter-long church was the largest then existing in the world. It had been destroyed in antiquity and its precise location lost to history. The Israeli archeologists were able to confirm their conjecture that the remains belonged to the Nea when they found a Greek inscription attributing the building to the munificence of Justinian.

A sixth-century mosaic map provided the clue to another important Byzantine discovery. The Madeba Map, found a century ago in a church across the Jordan, depicts the Holy Land and includes a large pictorial map of Jerusalem. At the heart of the city is shown a long street flanked by columns, the Cardo. Digging along the presumed alignment of the Cardo, archeologists uncovered a 22-meter-wide street lined by colonnades and store-fronts: the broad boulevard linking the two major churches in the city, the Holy Sepulcher and the Nea. Part of it has now been restored as a shopping arcade.

The third post-1967 major dig in Jerusalem was at the site of David's City, the narrow slope south of today's Old City on which King David had established the Israelite capital. The winds of history seemed to have swept the site clear of virtually any remains of that period except for a few small fragments of city wall, as a dozen archeological probes over the past century had attested. However, in a major excavation carried out during the 1980s, archeologists uncoverd the 18-meter-high base of a structure believed to have been the base of King Solomon's Citadel, as well as residential buildings and a wealth of material showing how the early Israelites lived. These finds included a flute carved out of a cow bone, handles of jugs imported from the island of Rhodes, and hundreds of full-breasted fertility figures, showing that Canaanite cults suprisingly still thrived even within a few hundred meters of the Temple, built to a stern God who permitted worship to no idols.

These archeological finds – whether they reflect a Christian, Jewish, Moslem or pagan past – belong to the story of man and are the common property of civilization. Together they tell a tale of a land which has survived every human folly, and yet has inspired mankind as none other.

126. The hot springs at Hamat Gadar attracted tens of thousands from all over the Roman Empire, who visited the sophisticated complex of baths, pools and theater built on this site on the southern slopes of the Golan near the Yarmuk River. Present-day visitors can also tour a large alligator farm that has been added to the Roman attractions.

127. The fourth-century synagogue at Bar Am in Upper Galilee is one of the best preserved of its kind in the country. Legend has it that Queen Esther was buried here. The exploits of the queen, and her uncle, Mordechai, recorded in the biblical scroll of Esther, are celebrated by Jews throughout the world in the joyous festival of Purim.

128.   An archeological excavation gets under way on a Galilean hilltop. The heart-shaped parts of columns suggest that the site might have been occupied by a second-to third-century synagogue.

129.   Herodium, the summer palace named after its builder, King Herod, in the Judaean Desert south-east of Bethlehem. From the top of the citadel, the signals of beacons lit in Jerusalem could be sighted and passed on to similar hilltop positions, thus facilitating speedy communication of important news, such as the approach of hostile forces or the advent of a festival.

130–132. Studies in arches. (top) An aqueduct built by the Turks as part of their fresh-water network, near Netanya. This town on the Mediterranean coast, today Israel's fifth biggest city, is a major resort and holiday center. It is also the hub of Israel's diamond-cutting industry – one of the largest in the world. (right) The Tombs of the Kings in Jerusalem's Sanhedria quarter. (far right) Burial caves in Jericho.

133. The winter palace of the Caliph Hisham ibn Abd al-Malik near Jericho is a magnificent example of eighth-century Arab architecture. This pillared courtyard stands in the center of the palace.

134. Part of the Roman baths at Hamat Gader.

135. The restored arched entrance leading to the Roman town of Caesarea.

136. The frescoes in the upper level of Herod's triple-stepped palace at Massada.

137–139.   Avdat, a Nabatean city in the Negev, dating from the second century B. C. This magnificent site, the most important Nabatean town in Israel, has given archeologists many clues to the Nabateans' successful cultivation of the virtually rainless southern desert. (left, below) This seventeenth-century Turkish fort occupies the site of Antipatris, a town built by King Herod on the site of the biblical town of Apheq, the scene of several major battles, including one where, in the eleventh century B. C. the Philistines captured the Ark of the Covenant from the defeated Israelites.

140.   The site of Mamshit (called Mampsis by the Greeks), a Nabatean town not far from the modern Negev development town of Dimona. Mamshit was conquered by the Moslems in 636 and never occupied again. Neglected for centuries, it was excavated early in the 1960s.

140

141. An anthropomorphic coffin in terracotta. Many of these Egyptian-made upright coffins, dating from the fourteenth and thirteenth centuries B. C., were found at Deir el-Balah in the Gaza Strip.

142. Christians from all over the world converge on the holy sites of Christianity during the major festivals. Each Friday, pious believers re-enact Christ's passion by retracing his path through the 14 Stations of the Cross on Jerusalem's Via Dolorosa, which ends inside the Church of the Holy Sepulcher.

143. Easter Sunday in Jerusalem. A passion play is re-enacted on the Via Dolorosa.

144. Nuns belonging to the Russian Orthodox Church participate in the Easter celebrations in Jerusalem.

145. A Friday morning procession, comprising pilgrims from abroad and local Arab Christians, wends its way along the Via Dolorosa.

146–149. The largest Christian Church in Israel is the Greek Orthodox, adherents of which are shown here during Easter Sunday observances in Jerusalem.

150.   The many-domed roof of the Church
of the Holy Sepulcher, the traditional site of
Calvary and the crucifixion.

151.   The spectacular, isolated monastery
of Mar Saba lies above a gorge in the
Judaean Desert. This Greek Orthodox
monastery, founded by St Sabas, was built
in the sixth century and is still occupied by
a few hermetic Greek monks.

152.   The sixth-century Greek Orthodox
Monastery of the Cross in central
Jerusalem. From this site, according to early
Christian tradition, the wood for Christ's
cross was cut.

155

153.   Christian pilgrims meditate upon Christ's temptation in the wilderness at the monastery of Karantal near Jericho. (The name is an Arabic derivation of the Latin Mons Quarantana, commemorating the 40 days of fasting observed by Jesus.)

154.   Midnight Mass marks the highpoint of the Christmas celebrations in the Franciscan basilica of the Church of the Nativity in Bethlehem.

155–157.   The Church of the Nativity in Bethlehem is shared by several Christian communities, each responsible for its own area. On the left, the Christmas processional in the Greek Orthodox section of the church: on the right and below, the Latin rite in the Roman Catholic section of the basilica.

158. One of the traditional sites of baptism. Thousands of devout Christian pilgrims from all over the world come to be baptized or re-baptized in the Jordan. At this point, the river flows into the Sea of Galilee.

159. An illumination depicting the Resurrection in an Armenian manuscript from the library of the Cathedral of Saint James, Jerusalem.

160, 161.   Mosaic floor from a second-century synagogue in Hammat, Tiberias, showing two menorahs (candelabra) flanking the Ark of the Covenant. The mosaic map on the right is in the Cardo, the restored central Byzantine street of Jerusalem. The original of this map (which shows the Cardo running across the center) is in the Jordanian town of Madeba.

162.   The grape harvest: a mosaic roundel from Beit Shearim.

ΙΑΠΟΛΙCΙΕΡΟΥCΑΛΗΜ

163. *A quiet courtyard within the closed Armenian Quarter of Jerusalem.*

164. *A Greek Orthodox woman at the church of Gethsemene.*

165. *Franciscans in a Palm Sunday procession walking toward the city from the Mount of Olives.*

164

168

166.   A view of the Temple Mount from
a window in the small church of Dominus
Flavit (where Jesus "wept over Jerusalem")
on the slopes of the Garden of Gethsemene.

167.   A theatrical performance in the
Knights' Halls, a series of passages in the
crypt of the great church of St Jean d'Acre.
The soaring Gothic archways of this church
in the Mediterranean city of Acre are the
setting of an annual festival of alternative
theater.

168.   A group of nuns at the arch of Ecce
Homo ("Behold the Man") in Jerusalem's
Christian Quarter.

169. One of the entrances to the Church of the Holy Sepulcher, Jerusalem, the traditional site of Calvary, Christ's passion and his final resting place, lies through a series of vaulted markets, dating from the Crusader period. These still sell a wealth of arts and crafts indigenous to the region, such as colored glass from Hebron, mother-of-pearl ritual objects from Bethlehem, olive-wood trinkets, handmade colored candles, and locally-embroidered dresses.

170. The 'Stone of Anointing' in the Church of the Holy Sepulcher. According to Christian tradition, it was on this stone slab that Jesus' body was anointed prior to burial, after it was brought down from the cross.

171, 172.   Two of the smaller Christian
communities in Jerusalem are the
Armenians – here preparing to set out on
their Easter procession, and the minuscule
Syrian Orthodox Church with just a few
hundred adherents, with its patriarch
residing in Damascus.

173. Communion in one of Jerusalem's innumerable churches. This one is the Church of Elias the Thesbite near the Garden of Gethsemene.

174. The high altar of the Latin basilica of St. Catherine in the Church of the Nativity, Bethlehem.

175.   At the Damascus Gate.

176.   A bedouin mother and child in their
Negev encampment.

177, 178.   Date palms and sand dunes near the Mediterranean coast at Israel's southernmost border with Egypt, near the town of el-Arish. Dates form an important cash crop for residents of the Gaza area.

*179, 180. Two Arab patriarchs in their
Judaean Desert home.*

181–183. The Jordan Valley. These villagers will have to travel many kilometers to reach home before sunset.

183

184. Women are an indispensable part of the labor force in Arab villages.

185. Yemenite Jewish women in traditional costume, including heavy silver jewelry. Before their mass immigration to Israel in 'Operation Magic Carpet' in 1948, Jews in Yemen were masters of the gold and silversmith's craft.

186

186–188.   A bedouin encampment near Jericho. In this traditional patriarchal society, women nevertheless play a major role. The family tents are made from wool collected from the black goats and woven by the women, who also make their own adornments and clothing.

8

189–192. These Arab farmers still till their fields with the ancestral skills and tools of their forebears. Modern farming methods are slowly taking the place of traditional ones, resulting in higher crop yields and less backbreaking work.

193

194

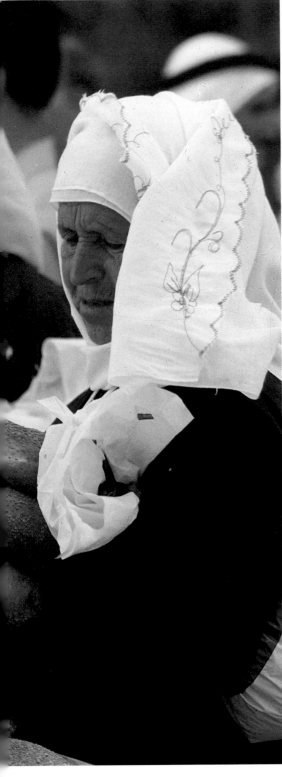

193–195.   Traditional Arab crafts embrace
a wide range of professions, from the sacred
to the mundane. The craftsman on the left
is hand-carving a delicate tracery of
arabesques in stone for the facing of
a mosque. The sesame-seed rolls and the
pancakes which will be filled with soft
cheese to make the delicacy of Ketaif call
for craftsmanship of a different order.

196. The splendid entrance to the Mosque of el-Jazzar in Acre. Built on the lines of Hagia Sophia in Constantinople, the mosque was embellished with pillars and marble floors brought from the plundered city of Caesarea.

197. Ramadan at the Dome of the Rock.

198, 199.   *Devout Moslem women in front of the blue-tiled Dome of the Rock during the month of Ramadan, when all pious Moslems refrain from eating and drinking from sun up to sundown every day.*

200.   *Thousands of devout Moslems prostrate themselves in the direction of the holy city of Mecca outside the Al-Aksa Mosque. The sebil or fountain in the center is used by the worshipers to wash their hands and feet before prayer.*

201.   *A packed congregation in the Al-Aksa Mosque, Jerusalem, listens to a Friday morning sermon delivered by an imam, a Moslem religious leader.*

202.   *Winding down a pathway on the Mount of Olives, Jerusalem, with the Temple Mount in the background.*

Chronology

c. 1550 B.C.	– Egyptian armies begin conquering Palestine.
Late 13th c. B.C.	– Israelite tribes occupy Transjordan and western Palestine, overcoming Canaanite vassal princes. End of Egyptian rule.
Early 12th c. B.C.	– Philistine invasion from the Aegean.
c. 1020 B.C.	– Saul becomes king of all Israel.
c. 1000 B.C.	– David succeeds Saul, crushes the Philistines, conquers the three Hebrew states of Transjordan, annexes the states of Aram.
c 961–922 B.C.	– Solomon organizes economic life, develops trade with Tyre and the Arabs, builds the Tample and royal palace in Jerusalem and many fortified towns.
c. 922 B.C.	– People of northern Israel revolt; the kingdom is divided into Israel and Judah. King Asa of Judah allies with Damascus, which wars with Israel.
738. B.C.	– Israel and Judah pay tribute to Assyria.
721 B.C.	– Assyria conquers Israel.
598 and 589 B.C.	– Jerusalem besieged by Babylonians.
August 587 B.C	– Nebuchadnezzar destroys Jerusalem; Judah devastated and almost depopulated.
539 B.C.	– Cyrus II of Persia conquers Babylonia and decrees the restoration of Judah.
330 B.C.	– Alexander the Great conquers Phoenicia; Palestine passes into Greek hands.
4th c. B.C.	– After the death of Alexander (323), Palestine falls to Ptolemy, founder of Egyptian Ptolemaic dynasty.
200 B.C.	– Palestine passes into the hands of the Greek Seleucid dynasty. Establishment of a philhellenic High Priest; many Jewish religious rites banned.
167 B.C.	– Altar of Zeus raised on the Temple Mount in Jerusalem, provoking resistance led by Judas Maccabaeus.
163 B.C.	– Agreement reached with the Seleucid regent, Tryphon. The Jews' religious liberty restored, but a Seleucid nominee is appointed High Priest. Another revolt follows; in 161 Judas is killed in battle.
63 B.C.	– Pompey takes Jerusalem; Judaea becomes a Roman vassal state.
40 B.C.	– Herod recognized by the Roman Senate as king of Judaea, reigns until 4 B.C., and rebuilds the Temple.
3 B.C.	– Augustus divides Palestine among Herod's three sons.
A.D. 6	– Direct Roman rule of Jerusalem through procurators.
A.D. 26–36	– Pontius Pilate is Roman procurator.
A.D. 44	– Entire kingdom becomes a procuratorial province.
A.D. 66	– Revolt of the Jews.
A.D. 70	– Fall of Jerusalem, the

Temple destroyed and the Jews dispersed.

A.D. 73 — All resistence ceases; Palestine becomes the Roman province of Judaea.

A.D. 132–135 — Bar-Kochba uprising. Jerusalem captured, but retaken by Julius Severus. After a last stand at Bethar (today Bittir), the rebels are defeated and slaughtered. Jerusalem becomes a Roman colony named Aelia Capitolina, a temple of Jupiter is raised on the site of the Jewish Temple, and Jews forbidden entry into the city.

A.D. 326 — After Emperor Constantine adopts Christianity as the state religion, his mother, Helena, comes to Jerusalem and erects churches and chapels on holy sites, including the Church of the Holy Sepulcher.

A.D. 395 — Partition of the Roman Empire, with Palestine falling to the share of the eastern emperor.

A.D. 636 — Moslem Arabs under Caliph Omar defeat Emperor Heraclius and take Palestine. Omar visits the Holy Mount (site of the Jewish Temple), cleans it, and builds a place of prayer.

A.D. 691 — Completion of the Kubbet es-Sakhrah, the Dome of the Rock, by Caliph Abd al-Malik.

A.D. 831 — Church of the Holy Sepulcher restored, but destroyed again some 100 years later.

1072 — Invasion of Palestine by Seljuk Turks.

1096 — First Crusade.

1099 — Capture of Jerusalem; Godfrey of Bouillon becomes ruler of Jerusalem.

1147 — Second Crusade led by kings of France and Germany; the Franks are compelled to make a treaty with Moslem leader Saladin.

1187 — After the battle of Hattin, Palestine restored to the Moslems.

1189 — Third Crusade, led by Frederick I of Germany and Richard Lionheart, proves ineffective, like the subsequent two Crusades.

1240 — Mongols from central Asia sweep through Galilee and capture Jerusalem, massacring and plundering. This is following by a period of Mameluke rule, and then a Tartar invasion.

1400 — Tamerlane of Mongolia devastates the land again.

1516 — Sultan Selim I defeats the Mamelukes; Palestine ruled by the Ottoman Turks for the next 400 years.

1798 — Napoleon attacks Acre, but is repulsed with the help of British warships.

1831 — Palestine comes under the government of the Albanian Mohammed Ali the Great, pasha of Egypt, who attempts to assert his independence of the Turkish sultan.

1840 — Re-establishment of Ottoman rule.

1896–7	– Theodor Herzl proposes the establishment of a Jewish state in Palestine. Foundation of the World Zionist Organization.
1914–1918	– World War I. Palestine the scene of a British campaign against Turkey. Jerusalem captured in 1917. Palestinian population decimated by warfare and hardships.
1917	– Balfour Declaration (November 2) favoring the establishment in Palestine of a national home for the Jewish people.
1920	– Sir Herbert Samuel named British high commissioner for Palestine. Start of British civilian administration.
1923	– League of Nations approves British mandatory rule. The Palestine constitution of August 10 falls short of Arab expectations and they boycott the elections.
1925	– Hebrew University opened on Mount Scopus near Jerusalem.
1929	– Serious Arab riots at Jerusalem, Hebron and Safad.
1930	– British government decides on closer control of Jewish Immigration but backs off after Zionist pressure. Arabs resentful.
1933	– Start of greatly increased immigration by Jews from Europe. Arabs demand independence and democratic self-government.

1936–38	– Arab revolt of unprecedented scope starts with general strike and turns into battles against British military detachments. Royal commission suggests partition of the country and termination of the mandate after a transitional period. Arabs reject the scheme and armed resistance continues. Arab leaders exiled.
1939	– Military reinforcements put down the rebellion. British promise an independent Palestine after ten years under a shared Jewish and Arab government.
1939–1945	– World War II. Palestinian Arabs remain neutral, Zionists opt to cooperate with the Allies. Zionists prepare for a postwar struggle by equipping their clandestine armed force, the Haganah.
1947	– Britain fails to achieve a compromise between Jews and Arabs, and refers the Palestine question to the United Nations. UN special committee recommends the partition of Palestine. Outbreak of a country-wide after Jewish-Arab guerilla struggle.
1948	– Many Arabs flee to neighboring countries; Britain termninates its mandate; on May 15, the State of Israel is proclaimed.

Index
of Names and Places

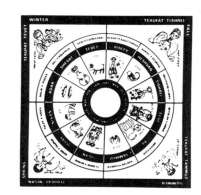